The Celts

EDITED BY

DR. JOSEPH RAFTERY

The Thomas Davis Lecture Series

Published in collaboration with
Radio Telefís Éireann
by
THE MERCIER PRESS
CORK and DUBLIN

Published for Radio Telifís Éireann
by The Mercier Press
Spring 1964
Reprinted 1969
Reprinted 1974
Reprinted 1976
Reprinted 1979
Reprinted 1985

ISBN 0 85342 852 2

This edition 1988

Printed by Litho Press Co., Midleton, Co. Cork.

CONTENTS

INTRODUCTION

EVERY autumn, winter, and spring since September 1953, Radio Éireann has been broadcasting half-hour lectures, named in honour of Thomas Davis. Inspired by one of his famous sayings, "Educate that you may be free," the aim of these lectures has been to provide in popular form what is best in Irish scholarship and the sciences.

Most of the lectures have been in series; many have been single broadcasts; some have been in English, some in Irish. In the comparatively short time that has passed since they were initiated, the lectures have dealt with many aspects and with many centuries of Irish social life, history, science and literature. The lecturers, distinguished for their special learning at home and abroad, have been drawn from many nations but mainly from Ireland.

The general titles of some of the series provide an idea of the variety and scope of the lectures: Early Irish Society; Saint Patrick; Ireland and Renaissance Europe; Irish Battles; Science and the Nation's Resources; Irish Folklore; The Land and the People; The Shaping of Modern Ireland; The Celts; and The Integrity of Yeats.

The talks presented herewith were delivered in Spring, 1960.

THE CELTIC LANGUAGES

THE word "Celtic" can, like the words "Irish" or "English", stand for a great number of different things, but when we use it linguistically the meaning is very restricted; it refers properly to one stage in the development of the Indo-European languages and that term will therefore have to be defined. If we compare Irish *aon*, *dó*, *trí*, with English *one*, *two*, *three*, or with Russian *odin*, *dva*, *tri*, it is plain that there must be some sort of relationship; if we compare any of these series with the same series in Finnish *yksi*, *kaksi*, *kolme*, it is equally plain that there is no relationship. Irish, English and Russian are ultimately traceable to a common parent language which, however, can only be deduced by comparisons of its descendants and we call that parent language Indo-European, since all the languages of Europe derive from it, with the unimportant exceptions of Finnish, Estonian, Hungarian and Basque, as well as Persian and the majority of the languages of northern India. This is an impressive list; in one sense it may be said that the Indo-Europeans have conquered the world linguistically, since the only non-Indo-European languages of any importance politically are Arabic and Chinese, neither of which is at the moment extending its influence. But in another and more important sense that statement is meaningless, since the Greeks and Hindus of 500 B.C. had no longer any memory of a common ancestry; although scholars are often amazed by the resemblances between the oldest examples of Greek and Sanskrit, those resemblances were not close enough for any sort of mutual comprehension. And, in passing, it might be said that we should not be too snobbish about the Indo-Europeans either, since

9

behind Indo-European, which we might very tentatively fix in time somewhere in the third millenium B.C., there must lie countless thousands of years of human speech; what we call Indo-European roots, simply because our evidence will take us back no further, must be derivatives of other roots in long-lost languages of which we will never know anything. Indo-European is the name we give to the earliest recognisable stage in one group of the languages of the world. To say that the Greeks or Hindus were Indo-Europeans is like saying that Frenchmen and Rumanians are ancient Romans; their languages are lineal descendants of that of the ancient Romans, but that is a very different matter.

Indo-European, then, which is a language whose existence is deduced but not directly demonstrated, developed into new languages, such as Greek, Germanic and Celtic; and here we come to another difficulty, since Greek is a language which we know from documents for most of the first millenium B.C., while Germanic and Celtic are as theoretical as Indo-European itself and are deduced from the existence of later languages such as Gothic, German and English for Germanic and Gaulish, Welsh and Irish for Celtic. When we attempt to reconstruct Celtic or Germanic, we are in rather the same position as if all records of Latin had been wiped out and we set out to reconstruct it from the speech of the Frenchmen, Italians, Spaniards and Rumanians of to-day. The results would certainly be strange—it has been demonstrated, for example, that we would not get even the numerals quite right and would completely fail with the declensions—but nevertheless we would get a product which would demonstrate the common origins of the Romance languages.

A serious attempt has been made to insert another theoretical stage of development between Celtic and Indo-European by postulating an Italo-Celtic unity from which Celtic on one hand and Italic on the other developed. Italic is another deduced language, the ancestor of Latin and its two neighbours, Oscan and Umbrian, both of which have left inscriptions which are long enough to give us a fair idea of their structure. One scholar who supported this theory very strongly was Antoine Meillet, who went so far as to speak of an "Italo-Celtic" nation which he would have placed in time about a thousand years before the oldest Italic evidence, that is, towards the end of the second millenium B.C. It is true that there are some striking parallels between the grammar of Latin and that of Old Irish and one phonetic point of resemblance has been given an entirely disproportionate amount of attention. This is the famous substitution of P for Q, which has given us such doubtful terms as "P" and "Q" Celts. The facts of the case are simple enough. There was a sound in Indo-European which gave qu (kw) in Latin and in the Irish of the Ogam inscriptions (in later Irish it became simply *c*), while in Oscan and Umbrian it became *p* and the same change happened in all the Celtic languages but Irish; so the number "four" is *quattuor* in Latin and *ceathair* in Irish, but *petora* in Oscan and *petor* in Gaulish. The Latin author Festus commented on this latter coincidence and some of the proponents of the Italo-Celtic unity were so struck by the agreement in this respect of Latin and Irish against Oscan and Gaulish that they were ready to accept the theory of a splitting of Italo-Celtic into P and Q dialects as an intermediate stage. But, strange as it may appear at first sight, the change from q to p is a reasonably common one—it is found, for example, in Greek, without that fact giving us any right to assume a special connection between Greek and Celtic. I do not think, in fact, that any serious scholar holds to P and Q branches of Italo-Celtic, and the whole concept has come under very severe fire, notably from Marstrander, who, after a study of the vocabulary of Latin on the one hand and of Irish and Welsh on the other, concluded that there could be no basis for Meillet's theory of an Italo-Celtic nation; I, personally, am convinced by his arguments and I think that, when working backwards from the linguistic material available, we can distinguish no intermediate grouping between Indo-European and Celtic.

The question naturally arises: "At what period, then, did the Celtic unity exist?" That question cannot, of course, be answered with any certainty and I would not like to go further than saying: "Sometime in the first half of the first millenium B.C." I will go a little further by saying that I have carried out, in a very amateurish way, a comparison of the vocabulary of Irish and Welsh, on the lines laid down by Swadesh, who believes that vocabulary has a constant rate of change and I arrived at a date of *circa* 700 B.C. for the period where the ancestors of Irish and Welsh began to diverge. I must emphasise that I have strong doubts about the validity of Swadesh's methods and that it is quite possible that I have not applied them correctly so that I do not offer this date as any more than a guess, but it at least lies in the area of probability.

As I have already said, we do not possess any direct knowledge of Common Celtic and, even in the second half of the first millenium B.C., our knowledge of the languages of the Celtic tribes is really very small. Thurneysen puts it very succinctly in the introduction to his grammar of Old Irish:

". . . Continental Celtic, often called Gaulish for short, the languages of the Celtic tribes in the two Gauls, the Iberian peninsula, Central Europe as far as the Black Sea, and Galatia in Asia Minor after the Celtic Galatians had settled there. None of these survived into the Middle Ages, and their records, although of great importance for the history of the Celtic languages, are very meagre. Gaulish texts survive only in some fifty inscriptions, most of them short and all, except for a few in Northern Italy, found in France. Apart from these we have only a number of personal, tribal and place names, together with some words regarded by ancient writers as Gaulish. . . ."

That statement of the situation leads us to the next question: "How is a Celtic language defined?" Obviously, in the first place, by phonetic criteria, since most of our material consists merely of names; we find certain correspondences such as the loss of the sound which we take to have been *p* in Indo-European, and the change of *e* into *i*, and the sum of these correspondences constitutes the evidence for the sound system of Common Celtic. Thus Irish has *athair* corresponding to Latin *pater* and *rí* corresponding to Latin *rex*, and Gaulish has *riges* corresponding to Latin *reges*. It would be helpful if we could call in morphological evidence as well, that is to say, grammatical forms, but the Continental evidence is too slight for that; the one thing we can be fairly sure of is that there was a genitive singular and nominative plural in -*i*, just like Latin *dominus*, *domini*—one of the arguments for the Italo-Celtic unity, of course. But otherwise the interpretation of Gaulish forms is uncertain, so that Old Irish remains our main source of evidence for Celtic morphology. Our third criterion, however, that of vocabulary, is a good deal better; there are many words which are distinctively Celtic such as *dúnon* "fort" (Irish *dún*), *uxellos* "high" (Irish *uasal*), *vindos* "white" (Irish *fionn*), *maros* "big" (Irish *mór*). When we hear a Gaulish name like *Nertomarus* it requires little thought to interpret it as *neartmhar* "strong", just as the tribal name *Bituriges* will readily yield the meaning "kings of the world" if we think of Irish *bith* "world" and *rí* "king". But, I need hardly say that only a small proportion of the words we have from Continental Celtic are as transparent as that and, indeed, it would be surprising if we could understand the vocabulary completely with nothing to help us but Irish and Welsh, for Gaulish must not be looked on as the ancestor of the modern Celtic languages, but rather as an early example of a branch which soon died. And, if we know little about Gaulish, we know even less about the other Celtic languages of the Continent or their relationships to one another; we cannot even be sure that Celtic-speaking peoples are meant when Classical writers use the names *Keltoi* or *Galatae*, for these ethnic names were used with considerable looseness—indeed, we do not know what *Keltoi* and *Galatae* meant originally, but there is no evidence that they are Celtic words or that any Celtic-speaking peoples ever called themselves by those names. That the Galatians were at one time Celtic-speaking is testified to only by a handful of proper names, for their few surviving inscriptions are in Greek, and it is difficult to take seriously the statement of St. Jerome that the Galatians of his time spoke a language which was almost the same as that of the Treveri, who gave their name to Trier in the Rhineland; it is hard to believe that this was not purely a historical statement, since it will be remembered that St. Jerome was writing in the fourth century A.D., when the Celtic dialects were on the point of extinction everywhere on the Continent of Europe. The latest date that is at all likely for the survival of a Celtic dialect is the sixth century, suggested by Hubschmied as the time when Alemannic replaced Gaulish in the Swiss Alps, but even this rests on very insecure evidence. To sum up, we can say that the presence of Celtic-speaking peoples is attested for several hundred years before and after the beginning of the Christian era, and for nearly every part of Europe except the far north, but of only one dialect, Gaulish, have we even a fragmentary knowledge.

However, the Celts left their mark. In a later chapter, Professor Tierney will tell you of the impression they made on the Greeks and Romans; I am concerned only with the linguistic side, but some of the words which classical writers learned from the Celts are worth mentioning. *Bardoi*, for example, whom Posidonius in the second century B.C. accurately described as "poets who deliver eulogies in song" and, of course, *druides* ; the wide extension of these terms indicates that the Celts had an individual and well-organised form of society.

The Romans noted, but did not borrow, these words; they did borrow a number of names of weapons, such as *lancea* and, what is rather more surprising, names of vehicles such as *carrus* and *carpentum*, which we have to the present day in "car" and "carpentry". What are even more interesting than the words which the Romans borrowed are those which found their way into the Germanic languages; in this case it was clearly the Celts who were the superiors culturally, for we find that the German word *Reich*, "kingdom", comes from the Celtic *rigion* and that *Amt*, "public office", comes from *ambactus* (incidentally the same words come into English through French and Italian as *rich* and *ambassador*). These loans into Germanic and Latin must be distinguished, of course, from the Celtic words which held on, so to speak, when former Celtic-speaking areas went over to German and Latin; there are few of these in standard German, but probably a fair number in Swiss German dialects, usually concerned, as might be expected, with agriculture and we find very much the same situation in French, where only a handful of words in the ordinary dictionary are of Celtic origin—*mouton*, "sheep", cognate with Irish *molt* and *ruche*, "beehive", cognate with Irish *rusc*, "bark of a tree" are two well-known examples—but a good number of words of probable Celtic origin turn up in the dialects.

Very little would be known about Celtic if it were not for the British Isles, though, as Eoin MacNeill pointed out many years ago, their name probably means originally the Pretanic, or Pictish, Isles, and the Picts were, in origin at least, not Celtic and their name later serves to indicate simply non-Celtic peoples, who may have been of diverse origins. When history begins, however, the British Isles are dominated by Celtic-speaking peoples and no direct evidence survives of older languages. The early state was simple enough; British was spoken in Britain and Irish in Ireland, though scholars prefer to call them Brythonic and Goidelic respectively. Now Brythonic has the sound P where Goidelic has Q and agrees with Gaulish in this, so that some people have concluded that Brythonic and Gaulish must have belonged originally to the same branch, while Goidelic belonged to another. As I have said before, this change of Q to P is quite a natural one and it is not by itself sufficient reason for making a new classification— it would not be reasonable, for example, to make Icelandic and English a special branch of the Germanic languages simply because they both keep the old sound *th* while the others have lost it. It is safer to regard Brythonic and Goidelic as languages which existed at the same time as Gaulish and which we reconstruct from the modern languages. We know, of course, of the existence of Brythonic from Roman sources, since Britain became a Roman province early in the Christian era, but Goidelic is much more difficult, for the first real list of Irish names comes from Ptolemy's Geography, compiled about 150 A.D., and the trouble is that hardly any names are identifiable, though one or two of them, like *Brigantes*, look Celtic enough. O'Rahilly attacked the problem boldly by assuming that the names were taken from the lost work of Pytheas and date from the fourth century B.C.; on this assumption he explained some of them as Brythonic and used this as evidence for his theory that the first Celts to come to Ireland were Brythonic. So far as I know, no scholars have accepted this ruthless re-dating; we are still faced with the strange picture of Ireland in the first or second century A.D. with few recognisable names—far fewer than in his description of Britain. O'Rahilly thought that this showed that the account of Ireland must be far older than that of Britain; it seems to me that it is just as probable that a description of Ireland was a good deal harder to get and that the travellers' tales were unreliable. Our first glimpse of Goidelic comes from the Ogam inscriptions, which, being merely scratches on stone, are impossible to date, but probably go back to the fourth century. From the fifth century onwards, Latin writing was known in Ireland as well as in Britain and documents in Irish were being written from the seventh century onwards and probably a little later in Welsh.

I have introduced the words "Irish" and "Welsh" in the last sentence; this corresponds to the appearance of a new type of language. As you will have noticed from the words I have quoted, Gaulish was a language, in the same stage of development as Greek or Latin, which had lost few internal syllables and none of the final ones, and Brythonic and Goidelic show the same stage; Irish and Welsh, on the other hand, had lost most of the final syllables and show considerable internal changes as well—*Nertomarus*, with four syllables, gives way to *nertmar* and *nerthfawr* with two, so that the difference is comparable to that between Latin on the one hand and the Romance languages on the other. This profound change took place in Goidelic some time after the beginning of the fourth century and before the end of the sixth and it is convenient to call the old language Goidelic and the new Irish; the change from Brythonic to Welsh is roughly contemporary. The results of these changes are far-reaching; as far as we know, the phonetic systems of Goidelic and Brythonic had been fairly close to each other, except for a few points like Brythonic *p* and *nt* where Goidelic had *c* and *dd*, but Irish and Welsh have been mutually incomprehensible ever since the period of change—that is, for at least fourteen hundred years. This by itself is an extraordinary thing, since no such differentiation had taken place in the Germanic or Slavonic languages at this time, and the Romance languages were barely beginning to develop from Latin. Not only that, but these new languages show a number of strange features, which are too often regarded as typically Celtic, in spite of the fact that there is no evidence that they existed in the earlier forms of the Celtic languages; it is, in my opinion, much safer to assume that they developed in these islands. Insular

Celtic, then, the only variety for which we have any reasonable documentation, is a very different thing from its Continental relatives.

I suppose the most striking innovation in insular Celtic is that of the initial mutations, which have few parallels in Europe at least; as the reader may know, the first consonant of a word in Irish and Welsh may change, or even disappear; what happens to it depends on the word that comes before it. This has really a fairly simple explanation. In all languages the phrase rather than the word is the basic unit of speech and in the insular Celtic languages the words of the phrase were so inseparable that phonetic changes took place inside the phrase in exactly the same way as inside a word. When we hear what is wrongly called "aspiration" in Irish—the Irish themselves had the better term *séimhiú*, "softening" or "lenition"—we know that this is based on a situation in which the word causing the lenition ended in a vowel, thus leaving the first consonant of the next word between two vowels, where it would be weakened. This internal weakening is common in many languages; for example, from Latin *liber*, "book", we get French *livre* and Irish *leabhar* where the *v* (or *w*) has been vocalised, and we find English *have* compared to German *haben*. Where the Celtic languages are unusual is in doing this in the *phrase* as well; we can take a very simple example from the article. You will remember that the forms of the article in French *un*, *une*, come from Latin *unus*, *una* ; the article in Celtic was different but had similar endings, which is all we are concerned with here. The final -*s* of the masculine preserved the following consonant and then disappeared when final syllables dropped, but the vowel of the feminine softened a following consonant before it disappeared itself; the endings -*os* and -*a* have been transformed into lack of change, or change, of a following consonant. In the same way a final -*n* brought about nasalisation 'eclipsis' before it dropped; the word for "ten" in Irish is *deich* and in Latin *decem*, but when we compare *deich mba* with Latin *decem botes* we see that Irish once had the second syllable, too.

The other big phonetic innovation concerns Irish only; that is the evolution of a system where every consonant has two varieties, velar and palatal, or broad and slender, as we call them traditionally, and here again this is due to the influence of those lost syllables, because the quality of the last consonant of a word in Old Irish depended on the quality of the vowel that had once followed it. So the declension of a word like *maqos, maqi*, "son", in Goidelic became *mac, maic*, in Old Irish, which achieved the feat of losing most of the old endings while still keeping the declension.

But, quite apart from phonetic changes of this kind, the insular languages show all sorts of innovations which distinguish them from the other Indo-European languages—things like conjugated prepositions, for example, or prepositional pronouns, as we call them in Irish; what is especially interesting about this class of words is that it exists both in Irish and Welsh, but that no amount of comparison of the Welsh and Irish forms will allow us to reconstruct common Celtic forms. I do not regard this as surprising, because I do not think that prepositional pronouns belong to Common Celtic, or that we would find them if we suddenly came across a big body of material in Gaulish; I think that there is every reason to believe that they were evolved separately in Ireland and Britain and that the only sense in which they can be called Celtic is that they were formed out of elements which in some cases show the development of the Indo-European languages which also characterised Gaulish and the other Continental languages of which I have been speaking. We have no reason to believe that the Celtic-speaking peoples had been in Britain and Ireland for any very great period before our historical evidence begins, or that the original invaders represented any more than a fairly thinly-spread ruling class, so that we should not regard Irish and Welsh as languages which were imported into their respective countries, but as languages which are really indigenous in the sense that they have grown up as the result of all the linguistic and social influences which have touched Ireland and Wales over more than two thousand years.

It remains only to glance at the history of the insular Celtic languages. The simple situation of Brythonic in Britain and Goidelic in Ireland did not last long; during the fifth century A.D. the Irish began to penetrate into British-speaking Scotland, and the English (if I may call them that for short) into the southern part of Britain, and soon British was everywhere on the retreat except in Wales and Cornwall; outside these territories the last stronghold was Strathclyde, where Cumbrian may have held out until the eleventh century. But if British lost heavily at home it made one new colony, for large numbers of British emigrated across the sea to what had once been the Celtic region of Armorica, displacing the Roman tongue by British and establishing what still bears the name of Brittany; this emigration took place in the fifth and sixth centuries, before the English power had, as yet, spread very widely in Britain and must be interpreted as a flight from the wrath to come rather than as a mass movement of refugees.

Irish, though subjected to influence from Scandinavian, French and English in turn, remained dominant in Ireland until the end of the sixteenth century, when the tide began to flow in favour of English; this had happened at a much earlier stage in Scotland, where, indeed, it can hardly be said that Irish had ever completely dominated. When Irish was introduced into the Isle of Man remains obscure, like so much else in Manx history, but it was still the vernacular in the seventeenth century. It will be noticed that I have used the word "Irish", since Scottish-Gaelic and Manx as separate dialects hardly go back farther than the twelfth or thirteenth centuries and do not appear in writing until the seventeenth century—and all still use some form of the word *Gaeilge* to describe themselves. Manx is dead now, and Scottish-Gaelic, though still vigorous, is almost entirely confined to the Hebrides. Of the Brythonic languages Cornish died in the eighteenth century; Breton has held its territory remarkably well, but has never been able to establish itself as a language of culture against French, and the vast majority of its speakers are literate only in French. Welsh, on the other hand, is firmly entrenched in the educational system, but is nevertheless losing ground to English; according to the last census the percentage of Welsh-speakers is now just under thirty. The Celtic languages are not dead, since at least two million people speak one or other of them as their native tongue, but, since none of them has succeeded in dominating a state, the vast majority of their speakers are perforce bilingual, and bilingualism under those conditions must ultimately lead to the loss of the less important language.

PROFESSOR DAVID GREENE

THE CELTS AND THE
CLASSICAL AUTHORS

IT is the object of this chapter to give a brief review of the information concerning the Celts, (also called Galatians and Gauls) which is to be found in the ancient Classical writers. This information is meagre for the early centuries and only gradually becomes somewhat fuller and more complete. It is, however, full of interest both because of its antiquity and because of its intrinsic value.

Archaeologists usually date the second period of the Iron Age, the La-Tène period, as beginning in the fifth century B.C. It is at about the beginning of this century, about 500 B.C., that the Celts first enter the glimmering dawn of history in the writings of Greek historians and ethnographers.

Our earliest information about Celtic tribes is contained, by a curious chance, in the *Ora Maritima* or *Coastal Survey* of Festus Rufus Avienus, who was proconsul of Africa in 366 A.D. The Greek original of this work was an account of coastal sailing from Cadiz to Marseilles in the early sixth century B.C. Its interest for us here is that it points to the existence of Celtic tribes on the North Sea, in France, and in South West Spain at that period. It gives the names of some Celtic tribes in Spain and provides an incorrect etymology of the native name of Ireland, calling it by the Greek name of "Hiera" that is, Sacred. It is agreeable to find that our earliest document thus confirms the findings of the archaeologists and linguists, who would put the arrival of Celts in central and south-western Spain as early as the seventh century B.C. and their existence on the Middle Rhine and in north-eastern and central France several centuries earlier still.

To continue with these early scraps of information: Hecataeus of Miletus, writing about 500 B.C. mentions Narbonne as a Celtic town, Marseilles as a Greek city, near Celtic territory, and Nyrax as a Celtic town. This last place was probably in Carinthia. Herodotus, writing fifty years later, mentions the Celts as living on the upper Danube, near the Pyrenees, and in farther Spain. In the fourth century B.C. our scraps become more numerous and more interesting; instead of mere names of tribes and cities we have references to national customs and to the psychology of the Celts. Xenophon in his *Greek History* tells us of Celts who were hired as mercenary soldiers by Dionysius of Syracuse. These men fought against the Thebans in the Peloponnese in the years 369 and 368 B.C. The philosopher Plato when writing soon afterwards on the self-control of the Spartans in regard to drinking wine, includes the Celts among a long list of barbarian peoples who indulge in drunkenness. It appears from the context, however, that this may be special pleading, and it should not be exaggerated.

It is in Aristotle, writing perhaps about 330 B.C. that we meet with observations of more real interest. He mentions that in warlike nations like Sparta, where women are given licence, or still worse, control, money is bound to be too highly esteemed, with the exception of the Celts and the other peoples which openly esteem homosexual relations. Aristotle is perhaps most interesting on the reckless Celtic bravery in battle. He says, "We have no word for the man who is excessively fearless; perhaps one may call such a man mad or bereft of feeling, who fears nothing, neither earthquakes nor waves, as they say of the Celts." Again, "It is not bravery to withstand fearful things through ignorance, for example, if through madness one were to withstand the onset of thunderbolts, and again, even if one understands how great the danger is, it is not bravery to withstand it through high-spiritedness, as when the Celts take

up arms to attack the waves; and in general the courage
of barbarians is compounded with high-spiritedness."
These and similar stories seem to be echoes of some
contemporary disaster caused by the flooding of the sea
into the area occupied by the Celts in the Low Countries.

In the historians of the late fourth century we have
references to the relations of the Celts with the Illyrians
and to their meeting with Alexander the Great on the
Danube, which reflect the military advance of the Celts
into the Balkans at the end of the century. In the early
third century the contemporary historians, such as
Hieronymus of Cardia and Demetrios of Byzantium
told of the great attack of the Celts or Galatians on
Greece, their retreat from Delphi and their advance into
Asia Minor. We have here a wealth of historical
information on the actual military events, on the
numbers of the Celts and their battle tactics, but what
catches our interest most is, perhaps, the blind fury of the
Celts as they fought to the death at the battle of
Thermopylae, or again the cavalry tactics, called
trimarcisia, the Celtic word for a horse being given as
"Marca."

A third-century poet says that the Gauls sacrifice their
prisoners to the gods by burning after a victory. The
historian Phylarchus tells how Ariamnes feasted all the
Galatians for a year and describes some of the Celtic
banquet-customs. The name of the Druids, as a kind of
barbarian philosophers, is first mentioned about 200 B.C.

In the second century B.C. we come to the historian
Polybius, who is the most voluminous author extant,
so far, on the Celts. It is in Polybius' history of the second
half of the third century B.C. that we feel that for the
first time the irresistible onward advance of the Celtic
tribes towards the south and east has been held in check.
The greatest period of Celtic advance had begun in the
early fourth century B.C. when the tribes moved south
from their ancient settlements on the Rhine and Danube.
Approaching Rome they took possession of Italy north

of the Apennines. By the middle of the century they had overcome the Illyrians on the Adriatic and were in touch with Macedonia and Greece. In the early third century a further rapid advance was made into Bulgaria, Thrace and Macedonia. After a partial defeat at Thermopylae they retreated northwards and founded a number of Balkan kingdoms, such as those of Belgrade and Adrianople. Remnants of their large armies crossed into Asia Minor and harassed large portions of the country for many decades until they were reduced to an uneasy subjection by Attalos I of Pergamon, in the twenties of the third century. It was at this period also, in the twenties of the third century, that the power of the Italian Celts was broken by the Romans at the battles of Telamon and Clastidium.

Polybius gives us numerous references to the Celts, particularly in his second and third books in regard to the Roman campaigns against the Gauls which I have just mentioned. The mass of his material, as is natural, concerns history and geography, but a few passages can be found of more general interest. Treating of Celtic living-conditions in Cisalpine Gaul he mentions such points as their beds of straw, their meat-eating, their pursuit of war and agriculture and simplicity of life and finally their institution of clientship. All these points turn up again in the later tradition about the Celts. In connection with the battle of Telamon in 225 B.C. we hear of the Celtic breeches and cloaks, their necklaces and bracelets, of their vanity and bravado in fighting naked, their head-hunting, their use of trumpets, their reckless courage and self-sacrifice in battle, and their mass suicide when defeated. A most interesting passage describes a series of duels among his Celtic prisoners, instituted by Hannibal on his arrival in Italy. The prize offered was a royal panoply, together with a horse and cloak. This account of the universal desire of the Celtic prisoners to take part, and their general acclaim of the vanquished dead no less than the victor throws a brilliant light on the war-psychology of the Celts. Although it lies outside the field of literature, I cannot refrain from mentioning here the large contemporary body of Greek and Greco-Roman art, dating from the third and second centuries B.C. and even later, which is the best illustration and confirmation of the Greek literary accounts of the Celts. These large sculptural groups were dedicated at the chief sites of the Greek world by the kings of Pergamon as an enduring record of their triumphs over these terrifying barbarian invaders. Many copies of these works, done by Greek or Roman artists, are to be seen in the museums of Western Europe, and most of us are familiar with the better copies such as the Ludovisi group in the Terme Museum or the Wounded Gaul in the Capitoline Museum in Rome. In these works of art all the physical elements of the literary record reappear, as though in exact confirmation of it. But it is on the higher level of ethos, of national character, that these sculptures show the Gauls most clearly, as depicted in defeat by their enemies. Ever since Homer, the Greeks had been quick to see and be moved by what was noble and ideal in the conduct of friend or foe. Through the eyes of the Greek artist of the third century B.C. we can still see the high Celtic spirit, the heroic spirit which Homer gives his heroes, whether in the grim savagery of the stress of battle, or in the stoical mass-suicide on defeat, showing that death was preferable to slavery.

It is well known, however, that by far the best and most comprehensive literary portrait of the Celts was provided in the work of the Stoic philosopher and historian, Poseidonios, who lived and worked in the first century B.C. In the rest of this chapter I will try to sketch the main points in the account of Poseidonios. The work of Poseidonios, which was contained in Book 23 of his *History*, is not extant, but his material on the Celts is reproduced in summary and with some changes and additions in three later Greek authors, the historian Diodorus Siculus, the geographer Strabo, and the writer of Miscellanies, Athenaeus. The dependence of these authors on Poseidonios for their Celtic material was proved beyond a doubt by Karl Müllenhoff and other scholars about a century ago. The similar material in Julius Caesar's *Gallic War* is apparently taken from Poseidonios without acknowledgement and with highly significant omissions and additions. The dependence of Caesar on Poseidonios has been the subject of more debate, but, in my opinion, it cannot be reasonably doubted. There is very little ethnographic material in later writers on the Celts which does not come from the four authors mentioned and ultimately from Poseidonios. This is true of the Roman prose-writers, of Cicero and Livy and many later authors such as Ammianus Marcellinus, and it is equally true of the poets such as Virgil, Lucan or Silius Italicus. It is only in the long lists of Celtic or Druidic cures which we find in Pliny's *Natural History* that we clearly come upon a source which is not Poseidonios. Poseidonios is, therefore, the central and crucial point in any discussion of the ancient Celts. The later tradition depends on him, and of the writers on Celtic matters before his time, of whom there were quite a number, nothing has survived except the fragments to which I have already referred, of which the most interesting and important are those of Aristotle and Polybius.

In order to clarify the position and practice of Poseidonios, I must here mention a few salient points about the tradition of Greek ethnography and historiography of which he formed a part. Since the fifth century B.C. the Greeks thought of the inhabitants of Northern Europe as being divided into two sections, the Scythians to the East and the Celts to the West. These two peoples were actually divided by many other tribes, including the Germanic tribes, but this latter fact became known only about 70 B.C. and was unknown to Poseidonios who wrote his history shortly before that date. He in fact regarded the tribes east of the Rhine as mainly a wilder and more barbarous kind of Celts.

The Greek historians, again, normally introduced ethnographic sketches to illuminate the narrative of historical events, particularly when a new or unknown people entered for the first time on the stage of history. Thus the occasion of the Celtic ethnography of Poseidonios was as an introduction to the first transalpine war against the Celts (125–121 B.C.) and stood in Book 23 of his *History*. There is no doubt that Poseidonios was the most eminent ethnographer of ancient times. Strabo tells us that his method was "to search for the true origins by studying the common qualities and family likenesses of nations," and this criterion is further defined as: language, way of life, bodily characters, geographical collocation, common names, all considered under the transforming influences of climate and of lapse of time acting either towards assimilation or towards dissimilation. Quite apart from his eminence as a natural scientist, as a historian and philosopher, we know that Poseidonios was well acquainted with Greek ethnographical writing, and that he lived for some period in Southern Gaul and collected his information about the Celts on the spot.

Is it possible to reconstruct what Poseidonios said about the Celts from these four later writers, three Greek and one Roman? The question is not easy to answer. His information, whether personal or derived from the earlier literature, was undoubtedly most accurate for the South of Gaul, and less so for the areas to the north and east. Further we may regard it as certain that he followed the traditional ethnographical schema (as we find it in Strabo and Diodorus) discussing first the land, its geography, economics, etc., and second the people, their physical and mental qualities and their way of life in the widest sense. Poseidonios was particularly expert in showing how the second of these factors depended on the first, that is, how the qualities of a people depend on their climatic and economic environment, thus following in the tradition of the great Hippocrates. Very probably these sections were preceded by another which treated of Celtic origins. This section would be of the highest possible interest to us, but of it, scarcely anything is certainly preserved.

Let us now glance briefly at our four sources. The first section, the geography of Gaul, is given with most detail by Strabo, as one would expect from a geographer. He gives, however, a greatly abbreviated version of the second section, on the people of Gaul. The historian Diodorus, on the other hand, curtails the geography radically, while in the ethnography proper, he also abbreviates ruthlessly, and omits important sections, while yet bringing us closest to the succession of themes in Poseidonios. Caesar, again, omits both geography and ethnography, confining himself to a brief discussion of the classes of political importance. Our last source, Athenaeus, does not purport to give a sketch of Poseidonios, but gives us, verbatim or nearly so, his account of Celtic banqueting and other customs.

In the time at my disposal it is impossible to analyse further the relationship of these sources to Poseidonios, and I must confine myself to quoting, with appropriate comment, three passages chosen for their particular interest to us because of the light they throw on the ancient Celts.

First a passage on Celtic food and drink, quoted verbatim by Athenaeus. It is, however, Celtic food and drink as seen by a superb social ethnologist, first in its physical background, then as an expression of a military hierarchy, and lastly in its social and economic framework:

"The Celts sit on dried grass and have their meals served up on wooden tables raised slightly above the earth. Their food consists of a small number of loaves of bread together with a large amount of meat, either boiled or roasted on charcoal or on spits. They partake of this in a cleanly but leonine fashion, raising up whole limbs in both hands and biting off the meat, while any part which is hard to tear off, they cut through with a small dagger which hangs attached to their sword-sheath in its own scabbard. Those who live beside the rivers or near the Mediterranean or Atlantic eat fish in addition, baked fish, that is, with the addition of salt, vinegar and cummin. They also use cummin in their drinks. They do not use olive oil because of its scarcity, and because of its unfamiliarity it appears unpleasant to them. When a large number dine together they sit around in a circle with the most influential man in the centre, like the leader of the chorus, whether he surpass the others in warlike skill, or nobility of family, or wealth. Beside him sits the host and next on either side the others in order of distinction. Their shieldsmen stand behind them, while their spearsmen are seated in a circle on the opposite side and feast in common like their lords. The servers bear around the drink in terracotta or silver jars like spouted cups. The trenchers on which they serve the food are also of these materials, while with others they are made of bronze, or are woven or wooden baskets. The drink of the wealthy classes is wine imported from Italy or from the territory of Marseilles. This is unadulterated, but sometimes a little water is added. The lower classes drink wheaten beer prepared with honey, but most people drink it plain. It is called corma. They use a common cup, drinking a little at a time, not more than a mouthful, but they do it rather frequently. The slave serves the cup towards the right, not towards the left."

Next a passage on Celtic battle-customs, from Diodorus, from among which the practice of head-hunting is strikingly confirmed by recent finds in Southern France:

"For their journeys and in battle they use two-horse chariots, the chariot carrying both charioteer and chieftain. When they meet with cavalry in the battle they cast their javelins at the enemy and then, descending from the chariot join battle with their swords. Some of them so far despise death that they descend to do battle, unclothed except for a girdle. They bring into battle, as their attendants, freemen chosen from among the poorer classes, whom they use as charioteers and shield-bearers in battle. When the armies are drawn up in battle-array they are wont to advance before the battle-line and to challenge the bravest of their opponents to single combat, at the same time brandishing before them their arms so as to terrify their foe. And when some one accepts their challenge to battle, they loudly recite the deeds of valour of their ancestors and proclaim their own valorous quality, at the same time abusing and making little of their opponent and generally attempting to rob him beforehand of his fighting spirit. They cut off the heads of enemies slain in battle and attach them to the necks of their horses. The blood-stained spoils they hand over to their attendants and carry off as booty, while striking up a paean and singing a song of victory, and they nail up these first fruits upon their houses just as do those who lay low wild animals in certain kinds of hunting. They embalm in cedar-oil the heads of the most distinguished enemies and preserve them carefully in a chest, and display them with pride to strangers, saying that, for this head, one of their ancestors, or his father, or the man himself, refused the offer of a large sum of money. They say that some of them boast that they refused the weight of the head in gold; thus displaying what is only a barbarous kind of magnanimity; for it is not a sign of nobility to refrain from selling the proofs of one's valour, it is rather true that it is bestial to continue one's hostility against a slain fellow-man."

And lastly a second passage from Diodorus on the Celtic temperament and the Celtic learned classes:

"Physically the Gauls are terrifying in appearance, with deep-sounding and very harsh voices. In conversation they use few words and speak in riddles, for the most part hinting at things and leaving a great deal to be understood. They frequently exaggerate with the aim of extolling themselves and diminishing the status of others. They are boasters and threateners and given to bombastic self-dramatization, and yet they are quick of mind and with good natural ability for learning. They have also lyric poets whom they call Bards. They sing to the accompaniment of instruments resembling lyres, sometimes a eulogy and sometimes a satire. They have also certain philosophers and theologians who are treated with special honour, whom they call Druids. They further make use of seers, thinking them worthy of praise. These latter by their augural observances and by the sacrifice of sacrificial animals can foretell the future and they hold all the people subject to them. In particular, when enquiring into matters of great import they have a strange and incredible custom; they devote to death a human being and stab him with a dagger in the region above the diaphragm, and when he has fallen they foretell the future from his fall and from the convulsions of his limbs and, moreover, from the spurting of the blood, placing their trust in some ancient and long-continued observation of these practices. Their custom is that no one should offer sacrifice without a philosopher; for they say that thanks should be offered to the gods by those skilled in the divine nature, as though they were people who can speak their language, and through them also they hold that benefits should be asked. And it is not only in the needs of peace but in war also that they carefully obey these men and their song-loving poets, and this is true not only of their friends but also of their enemies. For oftentimes as armies approach each other in line of battle with their swords drawn and their spears raised for the charge, these men come forth between them and stop the conflict, as though they had spellbound some kind of wild animals. Thus, even among the most savage barbarians anger yields to wisdom and Ares does homage to the Muses.

PROFESSOR JAMES J. TIERNEY

THE ARCHAEOLOGY OF THE
CONTINENTAL CELTS*

In the following discussion of the Continental Celts I should like to talk as an archaeologist and to leave to one side, the history of this people as revealed to us by Classical sources from the first mention of them to their final and complete incorporation in the Roman Empire under Caesar and Augustus. I shall attempt to make the archaeological remains tell their own story and only support their evidence by the written tradition where the possibility of important confirmation exists.

As a point of departure for our study I have selected a discovery made only a few years ago, one which occasioned much enthusiasm. This occurred in France, in the little village of Vix, on the upper Seine. It was a find which was widely and frequently publicised not only in the scientific journals but in daily newspapers and illustrated magazines.

Vix lies at the foot of a low, isolated height called Mont Lassois, the scene of excavations over a long period. These excavations have shown that the mountain repeatedly attracted men to settle there from late Stone Age times onwards. The site must, however, have been one of especial significance in the 2nd half of the 6th century B.C. At that time it was surrounded by a strong defensive wall within which innumerable sherds of Greek vessels were found, together with other settlement debris. These sherds prove that the inhabitants of Mont Lassois had extensive commercial contacts with the Mediterranean world. In addition, some burials with rich grave deposits, found in the immediate neighbourhood of the

---

*Translated from the German by the Editor.

mountain settlement, indicate clearly that we are here concerned with a group of people who were distinguished from their fellows by wealth and power: they must have been princes of a sort who dwelt on this spot.

The recent discovery, however, of the new grave, with unprecedentedly rich equipment, gave rise to great excitement. The skeleton of a young woman was found in a wooden chamber which, originally, was probably covered by a great tumulus. She lay on a bier provided by an ornamented, four-wheeled wagon. On her body lay several brooches, armlets and anklets and a string of stone and amber beads. The most significant single item of personal decoration, however, was a diadem of heavy gold, richly ornamented with, amongst other devices, a pair of winged horses which, in the fineness of their execution, betrayed the hand of a master schooled in the workshops of the south. Beside the body there stood a Greek vessel of bronze—a krater—of truly huge proportions, with figured ornament of the finest quality. Standing just 5 feet high, it can be stated that no vessel of this magnitude is known, although there are descriptions of such in Classical sources. Two Greek drinking vessels, made in Athens about 520 B.C., lay on the rim of the krater and, as well, there was a complete drinking set of bronze and silver vessels, including two bowls and a can certainly from Etruria.

These finds, then, show that we have to reckon, not only with trade relations with Greeks (who were probably inhabitants of the city of Massilia, the modern Marseilles and also lived along the Saône and Rhone valley), but also that the Etruscans participated in the commerce with Central Europe. This people had, by the end of the 6th century B.C., extended its power to the Po plains of Northern Italy; from here, passes through the central and western Alps provided contacts with the chieftains of the upper Seine.

Princely graves, like that at Vix, are known not only in eastern France but also in central Switzerland and south-western Germany. Unfortunately, most of these were uncovered a long time ago and were, in consequence, not as carefully investigated as science nowadays demands. Fortified sites of these richly caparisoned dead include Hohenasperg near Stuttgart and especially the Heuneburg on the upper Danube, where for a number of years excavation has been in progress with results similar to those from Mont Lassois. As well, many simple graves of the ordinary people are known; and all these finds together are included by archaeologists in what is known as the western Hallstatt province, called after Hallstatt in the Austrian Alps where valuable finds of this period were made. These finds are proof of a socially differentiated population which, to judge by its possession of such a quantity of valuable Greek and Etruscan material, must have been equal trading partners with these Mediterranean folk.

In spite of all this, however, we do not get any more detailed information about this population from ancient tradition. With reasonable probability, we can deduce from the reports of Greek historians alone that we are dealing with Celts. Hecataeus of Miletos, who lived at the end of the 6th and the beginning of the 5th century B.C., can have referred to these people only when he mentioned the existence of Celts in the hinterland of Massilia. Herodotos, who wrote his historical work about a half century later, mentions Celts at the source of the Danube; but a detailed description of the Celts, with which we can compare the results of archaeological research, is first made available to us at that moment when the Gauls break into Italy.

One may, perhaps, recall the report by Livy in which he describes how the Gauls pressed over the Alps into the valley of the Po, drove the Etruscans thence and settled themselves in their place. More briefly, if more factually, Polybius tells of the same events. Amongst the latest arrivals in northern Italy were the Boii, who occupied the territory south of the River Po and around

the modern Bologna, and the Senones, who established
themselves near the Adriatic coast in the area between
Rimini and Ancona. The Romans are said to have
become involved in the battle between the Senones and
the inhabitants of Clusium, the modern Chiusi. This it
was that led to Brennus's march on Rome in 387 B.C.,
when the city was destroyed and the siege of the capital
was lifted only after the payment of a heavy tribute. In
the next hundred years, the Gauls, time and again,
mounted plundering raids into the heart of central
Italy, until the Romans were eventually successful in
283 B.C., in defeating the Senones decisively and driving
them from their territory on the Adriatic coast. However,
it took much longer for the rest of the Gauls in northern
Italy to be subjugated by the Romans.

For our research into the history of the Celts in Italy,
the International Congress of Archaeology, held in
Bologna in 1871, was of the utmost importance. At that
time the great excavations, which gave such a fine
picture of the Etruscan past, were being conducted
within the confines of the city itself and somewhat south
of it, at Marzabotto in the Reno valley. Now, amongst
the many Etruscan finds, French scholars began to
recognise objects with which they were already familiar
from ancient graves in France, and especially in the
Champagne. As it was certain that recognisable weapons
and items of personal ornament belonged to Celts in
France, similar objects in Bologna could be accepted as
the legacy of the Gauls who had penetrated to Italy.
Once the character of these objects had been recognised
it became possible in the succeeding years to collect so
much material together that it is now possible to paint
a reasonably accurate picture of the Celtic occupation
of Northern Italy.

I should like to describe some graves, which were
uncovered at the end of the last century at Montefortino
and Filottrano in the neighbourhood of Ancona, and
which must be ascribed to the Senones. The dead were

buried in wooden coffins, which were sunk in the earth and often given the additional protection of a stone setting. Men were accompanied by those long swords of iron already well-known to us from the reports of classical writers. The dead also had spears, the iron tip and often the butt of which were preserved in the graves. Occasionally, a bronze or iron helmet was discovered. Though it is certain that these people had shields, it seems that, at the period in question, such had no metal mounts and the organic material of which they were comprised has completely disappeared.* In addition to weapons, men's graves also contained metal and pottery vessels, toilet implements and even spindle-whorls. Some of the women's graves were even richer: as well as drinking vessels and unguent and cosmetic jars they also contained great quantities of ornaments, generally including engraved bronze mirrors.

If we can accept the swords and spears of the men's graves as Celtic (the helmets belong to a type widespread in Italy and only rarely used by Celts), it is only now and then, through brooches and neck- and arm-rings, that we can detect the presence of Gaulish women. The earrings, the vast proportion of the collars and armlets and the rest of the grave goods do not differ in any way from similar objects found in Italo-Etruscan graves.

The decoration of the ornaments, too, resembles most closely that of Etruscan work and has only faint Celtic feeling. In Central Europe at this time a positive and easily recognisable Celtic art style flourished, but in the graves around Ancona there are only few objects which are ornamented in the typical Celtic manner. For example, in a man's grave at Filottrano there occurred, significantly enough, an ornamented, bronze sheath-mount and in a woman's grave in the same place there was found a neck-ring or torc, a form of ornament shown

---

*The only known example of wood and leather from all Europe was found recently in Littleton bog, Co. Tipperary.—*Editor*.

on Classical representations as *the* most typical item of personal ornament of the Gauls.

These truly Celtic fabrications will, however, scarcely have been produced in Italy, where the invaders were entirely absorbed by the strong Classical culture and their individuality suppressed. We know, from the middle Rhine, for instance, an exact parallel to the collar from Filottrano and it is to be assumed that that specimen came from the Rhine to Italy; likewise, the sheath mentioned above was probably made, not by one of the Senones in northern Italy, but by a Celt, north of the Alps and possibly in the Marne district of France.

The chronological position of the graves just described is securely established (by Greek pottery found in them) to the end of the 4th/beginning of the 3rd century B.C. The graves illustrate for us the rich and secure life of the Celts shortly before its destruction by the Romans. All the discoveries suggest that the Celts had become native to Italy and one would not recognise in them, any more, the strange and horrible foreigners who destroyed Rome under Brennus.

Now for some details about the invaders themselves. We know, of course, that they stood before Rome as early as 387 B.C. and we must, therefore, assume that it was somewhat earlier that they advanced into northern Italy, though the Classical authors assign contradictory dates to this event. This is, indeed, one of the thorniest of our research problems, for we have so far only few finds in Italy which can with any degree of certainty be dated to the beginning of the 4th century, B.C.: the hordes of Brennus cannot as yet be identified in the archaeological remains.

The great migration can be indicated only in a negative way. Amongst the Greek and Etruscan cities in the Po valley, made known to us through excavation, Spina, on the estuary, had certainly flourished for a long time when the Gauls made themselves masters of the land. The well-dated Greek pottery of Adria, the other great harbour, ceased about the thirties of the 5th century, B.C. and about the same time the importation of Greek wares into Numana near Ancona stopped. The only explanation of these facts must be the Gaulish attack. The Etruscan cemetries round Bologna, the most important city in the valley of the Po, were in use throughout the whole of the 5th century and grave-stones exist on which the struggles of the natives with the Celts are represented. They show quite clearly that, at the end of the 5th century, the city had to wage a war with the Gauls and that the Celtic migration into Italy was in full swing at this time.

In the eastern ports of the Mediterranean, too, the Classical writers tell us in circumstantial detail of great Celtic migrations. The earliest document refers to the time of Alexander the Great who, before he set out in 334 to conquer the Persian Empire after his battles with the Thracians and Illyrians, received delegates of these people together with representatives of the Celts. This shows that the Celts must already have penetrated into the northern Balkans. A half century later, after the collapse of the Kingdom of Lysimachos, Celtic warrior bands pressed into Thrace and Macedonia. In 279 they plundered Delphi and large bodies of them moved further afield to Asia Minor where they were for long the terror of the colonial Greek cities.

Archaeologically speaking, however, it is practically impossible to identify the Celts who moved to the east in contradistinction to those who settled in Italy. It may be taken for granted that the eastern Celts came quickly under the strong influence of southern culture, losing, thereby, their individuality, though one clear archaeological proof of their presence in Asia Minor is provided at Pergamon. There, amongst the reliefs of the sanctuary of Athena, built by King Eumenes II about 180 B.C. to commemorate a victory over peoples called *Galatae* by the Greeks, trophies are depicted which include typical Celtic weapons.

A strong and individual Celtic culture can be recognised only in central and western Europe, from the east coast of Spain to Hungary and Yugoslavia; discoveries in England and Ireland indicate that Celts also reached the shores of those islands. This culture, called La Tène after the place of discovery, on Neuenburg Lake in Switzerland, of a huge hoard of weapons, comprises typical weapons and brooches, ornaments and pottery, and everything associated with them which we know from cemeteries and settlements.

The original source of the La Tène culture is not confined to the area occupied by the Hallstatt Culture, of which I wrote at the beginning of this chapter. Those areas north of the Hallstatt territory, including the Champagne in France, the middle Rhine and Bohemia, appear to be more important. In this area, in the 5th and more rarely also in the 4th century B.C., rich graves came to light which are reminiscent in many details of the older chieftains' graves of the Hallstat Culture. The dead are buried under huge mounds; they are likewise placed on chariots, now, however, of the light, two-wheeled variety as opposed to the earlier four-wheeled type. Weapons are deposited with the dead and also rich ornaments, sometimes of precious metals, as well as drinking vessels manufactured in the south. These southern imports give us a lively picture of the commercial contacts the Celts had with the Etruscans before their attack on northern Italy. One can deduce that there were close connections between the trade from the south and the raids from the north.

How important the contact with the culture of the Mediterranean must have been for the Celts is, perhaps, demonstrated by the development of a new art style, of southern origin, in the citadels of the opulent chieftains whose wealthy graves we know. The ornamentation of the personal jewellery and the utility objects of the Hallstatt Period was geometrical. The artists and artificers of the La Tène epoch, however, took enthusiastically to foreign prototypes, some of which were brought to them from the east through the mediation of the neighbouring Scythian tribes; the most important influences, of course, were Greek and Etruscan. In spite of that, however, the rich figural art of the Greeks finds no echo. We do not know what it was that prevented the Celts from representing human beings, but true it is that it was only the rich Greek ornament of intertwined tendrils with palmettes and anthemion that is imitated. The plant character of southern ornament, however, is immediately lost amongst the Celts and curving, abstract shapes, whose origin can, only with difficulty, be recognised, take its place. These designs change constantly, they vary and have a charming ambiguity. A purely ornamental art of great beauty is born which, though brought to life by external influences, yet represents a tremendous achievement of the Celtic character. Though development in Central Europe is interrupted by the Roman conquest, it exercised a strong, if hidden, influence on provincial Roman art. In England and Ireland this Celtic art persists even through Roman imperial times and, indeed, at that time some of the finest Celtic objects were produced; it carried on in Ireland to contribute an important element to Early Christian art.

We have shown, from rich graves of the 5th and 4th centuries B.C., that in the Champagne, along the Middle Rhine and in Bohemia there existed local princelings whose centres of power were so important for the development of the La Tène culture. There are also, in the neighbouring territory to the South, where for the preceding century we have demonstrated the various establishments of the Hallstatt chieftains, graves with the typical Celtic swords, spears, brooches and so on. In this area, however, we do not find the dead, with rich grave goods, under burial mounds; rather are they placed in flat cemeteries in which no grave is more richly equipped than its fellows. Thus, not only in the art but also in the manner of burial, do we see a marked change in this area. In addition, the occupation of the Hallstatt citadels, of which excavation has told us much, ceases with the beginning of the La Tène culture. This suggests a great social change in this area which had been completed before the beginning of the major Celtic migration. We cannot identify the leaders of these Celtic migrations through their graves; and the graves of the later lords who built the great defended seats, the *oppida* of which Caesar writes, or of the nobles such as Orgetorix or Dumnorix, are also unknown. Everywhere in central Europe the simple grave in the earth gradually becomes the dominant type and the objects deposited with the dead became scarcer throughout the La Tène period and, consequently, of less significance in the archaeological record.

It is not only the poverty of the graves that prevents our getting an adequate picture of later La Tène times: the great cities, the so-called *oppida*, of which we know a great number, are so extensive that, so far, only relatively tiny areas could be excavated scientifically. Important investigations were carried out already last century at the instigation of Napoleon III. In order to write his history of Caesar he had excavations made at Bibracte, Gergovia and especially at Alesia, the centre of the final Celtic resistance to Caesar. At that site the Roman barracks and fortification trenches were discovered and traces of the Celtic city were found, though largely destroyed by later buildings of Roman times.

A modern scientific excavation of an *oppidum* has been in progress for some years. This is at Manching near Ingolstadt in Bavaria, formerly the chief centre of the Vindels. We have as yet, however, only brief reports of the results. We can, therefore, not say more than, that Caesar's descriptions of the *oppida* are, in many details borne out and even supplemented by the results of the excavations.

I should now like to conclude by reverting briefly

to the origin of the Celts. We have described the La Tène culture as *the* Celtic culture. Its bearers did not immigrate into Central Europe in the 5th century B.C.; but rather can it be said that the La Tène culture bonded together, into a unity, the various peoples who lived there. I have suggested as one of their predecessors, which we may certainly describe as Celtic, the people of the western Hallstatt culture. I have given Hecataeus as a reference for this, when about 500 B.C. he talks of Celts. We may now, however, by virtue of Spanish discoveries, look upon the bearers of the Hallstatt Culture as early Celts.

Classical writings tell us repeatedly that the Meseta in the centre and the west of the Iberian Peninsula was occupied by Celts. In spite of this statement, however, a definite La Tène culture has never been identified in those regions; a Hallstatt culture has.

We have mentioned that Eastern France, central Switzerland and southern Germany formed the essential core of the western Hallstatt culture area. At the end of the 6th century B.C., typical Hallstatt forms are suddenly found far beyond this region. They occur as isolated specimens in the south-eastern Alps or even further away in northern Germany, though these stray objects may have been due to trading contacts. At the end of the 6th century, however, we find whole cemeteries of this culture in the Champagne. At the beginning of the 5th century we find further Hallstatt forms, such as typical fibulae, in southern France and, in one district in Iberia, we find the local culture changed to a Hallstatt complex whichcontinued in unbroken tradition there for hundreds of years. If there were not already Celts of some sort in the peninsula, it can only have been the introduction of the powerful Hallstatt culture which made Celtic large tracts of Spain and Portugal.

The great expansion of the Hallstatt people to western Europe can be explained only through great migrations about which, of course, we know nothing from written sources. These older Celtic migrations caused revolutionary changes, not only over large areas of the Continent, but they must have affected England and Ireland also. The upheavals, at the end of the 6th and beginning of the 5th century B.C., on the Continent, must have been responsible for the appearance in Britain of the first Iron Age settlers, the so-called Iron Age A people. Though individual population groups from the territory of the La Tène culture came from the Continent at later stages, it seems that it was these earliest Iron Age peoples who first laid the foundations of the Celtic settlement of the western islands.*

DR. OTTO-HERMAN FREY

---

*This chapter was prepared as a radio talk in 1959. Since then the investigation of the late Celtic *oppida* has made considerable advances; not only are more precise reports on Manching available but from Czechoslovakia have come the results of important research. These cannot, however, be dealt with here.

THE ARCHAEOLOGY OF THE CELTS IN IRELAND

In the earlier studies here we have learned something of the Celtic language, of the views held about Celtic-speaking people by Classical writers and of Celtic material remains on the Continent. A picture has slowly been emerging of a far-flung people with a linguistic, a cultural and a political unity. It seems proper to designate these people "Celts" even if the word can have no certain ethnic significance.

The Continental Celts possessed a material culture of high degree which is characterised above all by the new art style, developed by the craftsmen of rich overlords out of Greek and Etruscan fashions and motives. The chieftains were buried in chariots in graves under high mounds and, in life, they built impressive fortifications on high land. All this should be reproduced in the new homelands in the west but, when we come to scrutinise the facts, certain difficulties become, at once, apparent.

The major difficulty, perhaps, lies in the fact that, once agriculture had become established in Ireland, there was little substantial change in the fundamental way-of-life of our ancestors. There were, indeed, accretions to the cultural content but at no stage can one discern in the archaeological record, such an overwhelming cultural change as to allow of the interpretation that one population was completely submerged in another new one, or completely destroyed by it.

No one can yet say—it may never be possible to know—*when* the Celtic language first reached Ireland. On the Continent, Celts can be traced back into the early centuries of the first millennium B.C., into a period of uncertainty and upheaval. By about 500 B.C., however,

this time of unrest had come to a climax all over Europe
and large communities, chief amongst them the Celts,
began to take on the recognisable dimensions by which
they were to be known in history. For reasons we do
not yet fully understand, these Celts of Europe began
gradually to burst from the cramping bounds of the area
in which we first encounter them. They swept down on
Spain, on Belgium, or northern Italy; they even sacked
Rome. They were a vigorous folk, full of enterprise and
initiative and it need not be wondered at, that in places
where no Continental Celt may have ever set his foot,
the influence of his culture could be felt.

This seems, in large measure, to be true of Ireland.
Here, for some 1,500 years or more—a period known to
archaeologists as the Bronze Age—there existed a
culture, with an economic structure and a social organisation, of no mean order. This was conditioned by the
possession of great flocks and herds, of large quantities
of gold and copper and by far-flung commercial activities,
reaching even to the ends of the then known world.
Technologically, the Bronze Age Irish excelled; the
craftsmen of the time understood well how to ornament
the objects they produced, whether these were items of
daily domestic use, such as axes and daggers, or of
personal adornment, or of ritual significance.

But, with all that, it is difficult to see any new *creative*
spirit in the cultural ensemble of the Bronze Age. Types
of objects and ornamental designs had become stereo-
typed: the handbook of artistic motives was written and
the craftsmen used it conservatively, for generations.

The new techniques of pollen analysis and Carbon 14
dating indicate that the culture of the Bronze Age
continued in Ireland, at least until the last centuries
B.C., even down to the birth of Christ, that is, that the
basic living conditions of the island as a whole did not
change radically. However, the period of Continental
unrest, to which reference has been made, coupled with
some degree of climatic deterioration, did not leave

Ireland unaffected. At first tentatively, we see in the archaeological record an awareness of the tensions of the outside world. From about 650 B.C. onwards, new styles and types of objects began to be known in our country and these, though in the main fabricated here, were based on foreign models. Chief amongst these are the massive gold ornaments of the Late Bronze Age, the collars, the bracelets, the dress fasteners. There were, though in limited numbers, new types of swords, new shields, new personal ornaments, all imported from outside or copied from external prototypes. But these were, as yet, only items that came to us in the normal course of trade or cultural relations. It is not until about the 3rd century B.C. that anything so definite as a new culture, in the archaeological sense, can be discerned in Ireland. This is the Irish counterpart of the La Tène culture which characterised the Celts of the Continent. At this stage it seems reasonable to talk of Celts in Ireland.

As I have said, however, there is evidence to show that the indigenous culture of the Bronze Age still continued; and the body of La Tène material in the country is so limited that one can, in the present state of our knowledge, hardly do more than consider the incursions of minor groups.

The period in which the La Tène culture flourished is known in the literature as the Early Iron Age in Ireland and, as the name implies, a new metal—iron—had been exploited for the production of most objects of everyday use, bronze becoming more expensive and being, in the main, reserved for ornamental use.

When the knowledge of iron-working first reached Ireland, the influence of the old Bronze Age people was still strong and some socketed iron axeheads, for instance, made in the old fashion of bronze implements, serve only to stress the continuity of tradition. Some bronze buckets, imported from the Celtic areas of the Continent, were provided with new ring-handles in the manner of the native Bronze Age cauldrons. Gradually, however, the experimental stage was passed and by the last centuries B.C., an iron-using economy was common over Ireland.

In round figures the Early Iron Age in Ireland—that period during which we can, for the first time, recognise Celtic influence in the country—may be said to begin about 300 B.C. It continued, with much artistic development, until about 450 A.D.

A careful study of this long period, covering a millennium, shows, as we might expect, that sub-divisions are possible, though it cannot yet be stated when the various sub-periods began or ended. Thus, it is clear from an analysis of stylistic details that the earliest period, covering perhaps the third and second centuries B.C., stood in direct and close relationship with the Continent; soon the Irish genius began to assert itself and the new ideas began to be so changed that the original designs can only with difficulty be ascertained. A new provincial culture developed which was soon quite distinct from that of the homeland whence it sprang. Not long afterwards, perhaps from about 100 A.D. onwards, Ireland came increasingly into contact with the Roman world and there soon developed a distinctively Irish culture, with elements derived from the technological skills of the Bronze Age artificers, from the Celts of the Continent and from the imperial civilisation of the Romans.

What does archaeology reveal to us of the people of this distant epoch in Ireland? We know, as this is a "text-aided" period, something of the distribution of Celtic tribes in Ireland and Britain about the birth of Christ; from graves in England some chariots have being recovered which prove the Continental parentage of at least one of the tribes mentioned—the Parisii. Chariot-graves, however, have not, so far, been recorded for Ireland and it is true to say that we cannot, as yet, identify, culturally, any of the population groups mentioned, for instance, by Ptolemy. Apart from that, however, archaeology gives us some idea of the habitations of the time, of the methods of burial and of the general economy of the period.

How the un-free members of the community lived, we do not know; but independent farmers and wealthier overlords occupied houses surrounded by banks of earth—called *ráth, dún* or *lios* in Irish—or by dry-built walls of stone—the *cathair* or *caiseal* of the literature; in marshy land and on the edges of lakes *crannogs* were still being built for the use of free families.

One site, that was excavated about twenty years ago at Turoe, Co. Galway, was a ring-fort or *rath*. It consisted of a circular area, about 90 feet in diameter, surrounded by an earthen bank, lined on the inner face by a dry-built wall of local stone. Into this inner space there opened a wide gateway, facing a causeway over a deep-sided trench or *fosse*, which was hollowed out of the living rock and which ran round the outside of the bank. Within the homestead the evidence of occupation was plentiful. At one place there was a cobbled floor and on this there were piles of turf-ash and a small hearth, with two compartments, built of stone flags. There was a narrow drainage trench leading out of this habitation area, but there was no indication of the nature of the houses that once stood in this portion of the site. One large central post-hole in the fort may point to the former existence of a circular hut with a thatched roof, supported on the walls and on a heavy timber post in the middle; but, as much of the internal area had been disturbed before the excavation was undertaken, it was not found possible to arrive at any satisfactory conclusion about such a structure. Just inside the gate, however, there was a series of large post-holes, which showed that the wooden uprights that once stood in them were of an appreciable size. The building for which they were used must have been a lean-to structure against the dry-stone bank of the fort.

Many objects of domestic use came to light during the

excavation of the farmhouse, for such it was; personal ornaments were also found, but the nature of the soil precluded the recovery of objects of wood, leather, pottery or textile. Scattered through the soil at all levels were large quantities of animal bones, including ox, pig, sheep, horse (of the so-called Celtic Pony type), dog, wolf, fox, badger, hare, and Red Deer. No bird bones were found. The ox bones formed about 80% of the total bulk, a fact which gives us an interesting picture of the manner of men these Turoe farmers were.

Established on the land, a large proportion of their time must have been devoted to the tending of large herds of cattle. These animals were used extensively in the daily diet, which must also have included bread and probably porridge. What their fruit and condiments were, we do not know, nor whether they used butter or honey; the few bones of wild animals and the complete absence of bird bones indicate that hunting and fowling formed only a small part of their activities, a surprising result of the excavation, for the somewhat romanticised references in the literature of a slightly later date suggest a noble warrior class, which spent long periods at the chase. We do not know how the people of Turoe clothed themselves, but we do know that they fastened their garments with small iron brooches similar to the safety-pins of modern times. The complete absence of weapons, whether offensive or defensive, suggests a farming family, not to any degree unlike that on a small Irish farm of the present day.

The ring-fort and the stone-built cashel were representative of the normal homesteads of the farming communities of early Celtic Ireland; some were small, encompassing the farm buildings and the dwelling house of a single family, others were larger, as befitting the status and the economic obligations of the bigger farmer or of the landed nobility. Attached to such forts were the fields in which the crops were grown and some of these may still be observed in the countryside.

Some of the people of these early centuries lived in *crannogs* also—that is, on artificial islands built in the shallow waters near the shores of lakes or on the swampy, reed-grown banks themselves. What the underlying motive for the selection of such apparently uncomfortable places was, we do not know, but originally it must have been dictated by the necessity for defence and protection.

One of these *crannogs* was excavated during recent years at Lough Gara in County Sligo. The occupation of the site began at the time of the first tentative exploitation of iron in Ireland and, mixed with the objects of bronze, tin and gold, of the native tradition, a few crudely forged implements of iron came to light. This early phase of occupation was ended suddenly by the rising of the waters of the lake and it seems that the lakeside settlement was left derelict for a long time. It was reoccupied, however, by a family of farmers who established themselves there in the 2nd century, A.D. They levelled the surface of the small island by piling large stones on it. On this solid substructure they built a large circular house, whose walls were made of upright timbers round which wicker rods were woven. They were then plastered inside and out with mud and the roof, it must be assumed, was thatched. The floor of the house was paved with large flagstones which were covered with a clean, white gravel. On this, in the centre, the fire was lighted. It was a simple, open hearth without protection of any sort and the many layers of ash, clay and charcoal of which it was composed afforded evidence of long and continuous occupation. In and around the house and between its walls and the stout palisade surrounding the *crannog*, many objects were found which threw much light on the living conditions and the economy of the inhabitants. There were iron knives and small iron pans, pieces of large bronze cauldrons, spindle-whorls, beads and combs of bone and horn, often pleasantly decorated; there were pins and necklets of bronze, weaving tablets of bone and wood and many pieces of textiles; there were wooden vessels of many sorts and a wooden ox-yoke gave some suggestion of the farming proclivities of these *crannog*-dwellers; clay moulds and tiny, triangular crucibles showed that metal-working was carried on on the site, while many quern-stones proved that the people were farmers, who must have garnered their grain crops on the rich land surrounding the lake; several arrowheads of flint as well as portion of an iron sword and two iron spearheads gave some indication of the offensive and defensive weapons in use at the time.

Few sites such as that just described have been excavated; indeed, our knowledge of the settlement archaeology of the time when Ireland was being brought within the domain of Celtic civilisation is very limited.

Equally meagre is our information about burial practices. Cremation was in vogue in certain parts of the country. At Carrowjames, Co. Mayo, for instance, a small cemetery of nine, low, earthen burial mounds was excavated and it was found that six of them could be dated to the Iron Age. In them there were many small pits in which the cremated remains of the dead were interred. No pottery was recovered, in sharp contrast to the funerary customs of the Bronze Age, but with practically every burial there were deposited small offerings, such as ornamental glass beads in several colours, cast bronze rings, small bronze studs and flint arrowheads.

Burial by inhumation, also during the early Celtic period in Ireland, is attested by a whole series of unburned skeletons which have come to light throughout the country, interred in what are known as Long Stone Cists. While it seems likely that some of these may date to the early years of Christianity in Ireland, it is probable that most of them belong to the pagan centuries. In the tombs, which are built of thin slabs and are usually about 6 feet long, the bodies were extended at full length, sometimes orientated East-West, sometimes North-South. Most of these graves occur in the flat earth without any superficial distinguishing marks; sometimes they are inserted into natural gravel ridges or into sand dunes by the sea shore. In many instances they occur singly in the manner of so many burials of the Bronze Age, but often large cemeteries occur.

Though the information about the Early Iron Age— and thus of the early Celtic period in Ireland—which is provided by settlement archaeology and burials, is restricted, many sporadic finds throughout the country assist us in filling in gaps in the background details. The swords used by the people were forged of iron. They were short and double-edged and were provided with a cross-guard of cast bronze, often ornamented with pleasing designs. The hilt plates are usually missing, but in one instance, from Lough Gur, County Limerick, the haft was made from a carefully worked sheep's bone. These swords were carried in sheaths, made of two thin plates of bronze, held in position by binding strips along the edges and finished off at the bottom by cast bronze chapes, which take the fanciful shapes of stylised animal heads, the eyes of which are simulated by roundels of red enamel. The side plates of the scabbards are decorated with a variety of patterns, lightly incised into the thin metal. The patterns are all peculiarly insular, but betray the debt they owe to the Continental homeland whence they ultimately sprang. These designs consist of S- and C-curves and spirals, zig-zag lines and, above all, of a pattern of groups of straight lines engraved at right angles to each other and filling in open spaces round the spirals. This motif is known as "basketry work" and is characteristic of a whole group of Iron Age bronzes in Britain.

Occasionally, bridle-bits of bronze are found alone, but generally they are found in pairs, and in several instances, for example at Attymon, Co. Galway, a pair of bits has come to light together with two peculiar, spur-shaped objects called bridle pendants. In general, these bits and pendants carry, on their broad faces, ornament which consists of thin-stemmed curves and spirals and trumpet designs and basketry. The frequency with which these horse-trappings are found in pairs suggests that they formed the driving equipment of pairs of horses yoked to one vehicle, possibly the chariot of a hero.

Personal ornament is well represented amongst the material of the Iron Age. There are many fibulae or safety-pin brooches of bronze, all decorated. One of them, from the famous centre of the northern kingdom, Emhain Macha near Armagh, is of particular interest, in that the manner of fixing the pin to the bow of the brooch represents, perhaps, the earliest known example of the ball-socket principle. That this is characteristically Irish, is shown by the discovery of other similar specimens as far apart as Donegal, Armagh and Galway.

The variety of objects preserved to us from this distant period, together with the richness of ornament which was lavished on them, suggests a community of considerable wealth and social organisation. Such a society must have had some form of religious observance or ritual organisation and some evidence for this is provided in the archaeological record. At the ring-fort of Turoe there once stood an erect block of granite, ornamented over its whole surface by a grouping of asymmetrical spirals and curves, together with a triskele and an incised step pattern. This stone belongs to a very early phase of the Iron Age in Ireland and is paralleled by three further decorated and free-standing stones, at Castlestrange, Co. Roscommon, Killycluggin, Co. Cavan, and Mullaghmast, Co. Kildare. In ornament they are close to a group in Brittany and have cultural connections, too, with the Rhineland. In Celtic France, and especially at the famous sanctuary of Roquepertuse, there are many representations of two-faced and two-headed gods; in Ireland, at Boa Island, Co. Fermanagh, and at Kilnaboy, Co. Clare, one finds similar effigies in stone, while the well-known three-faced heads from Corleck, Co. Cavan, and Woodlands, Co. Donegal, belong to a widespread group in Celtic Europe.

From the material remains, we thus get a picture of a farming society in Ireland in early Celtic times, with great emphasis on stock-raising, of a people with enough wealth to be able to afford valuable personal adornment, of a folk with specialised crafts and with an economic surplus sufficient to support non-producers. We see, furthermore, that this people had very close connections, both with the neighbouring island and with the Continent and *that* from the early days of the development of the Celtic La Tène culture in the homeland. In Ireland itself, the archaeological material allows us to see, though as yet only vaguely, two distinctive provinces in the Iron Age, one concentrated in the west and with extensions to the Central Plain and another situated in the north of the country; the epic tale of the Iron Age, *Táin Bó Cuailgne*, coincides exactly in the distribution of its personnel with the archaeological evidence. An appraisal of this evidence suggests that the new and vigorous Celtic culture of the Iron Age, with its new art forms, its greater emphasis on the use of iron and its religious ideas, came to us, in the main directly from the Continent, along the old Atlantic Trade Route to the west of Ireland, whence it spread east and north-eastwards over the land.

It is, thus, obvious from many sources that this early Celtic period in Ireland was one of impressive creative activity, both artistically and politically. It was a dynamic time when Ireland, far from being cut off from the outside world, was as closely connected therewith as ever before. It was a time of colonial expansion, of aesthetic endeavour and of spiritual content, a heroic period to which may be attributed some of the finest of our earliest literature such as the tale of the *Táin* already mentioned, which has been described by one authority as "the wildest and most fascinating saga not only of the entire Celtic world, but even of all western Europe."

The degree of civilisation of the people of Ireland during the last centuries B.C. and the first centuries A.D. was very advanced; so much so, indeed, that the combination of the established Iron Age culture with the new ideas which Christianity brought in its train rendered inevitable, it seems to me, the development of an art and a spiritual mission which were destined to become in time the wonder of the western world.

DR. JOSEPH RAFTERY

CELTIC RELIGION AND CELTIC SOCIETY

In discussing the religion and the social organisation of the Celtic peoples, I shall begin with religion. It is important to reflect, at the outset, that we must not think in terms of the great world religions, of our own Christian faith with its philosophy and theology and a highly developed ethical and moral doctrine of which the ideal of charity is the perfect expression. Nor even of Mohamedanism which owes so much to the Old Testament, nor of Hinduism or the nobler Buddhist form of Indian religion. We are dealing here with primitive magic, for which modern analogies would most readily be found in Africa or among the hill-tribes of India or the still pagan tribes of North America; although the general culture of the Celts of Gaul was higher than that statement implies, judged by their achievement in decorative art. They were heirs to common Indo-European traditions. Indeed an analogy can also be found with the cult of Poseidon and Demeter in Ancient Greece, as we shall see.

Our earliest information is about the Celts on the Continent, about the Gauls, for the Welsh and Irish sources date only from the Middle Ages. Caesar tells us that the Gauls were much given to religion, and he adds that they had a special devotion to Mercury as the inventor of all the arts and crafts, and the patron of travellers and merchants, and that they also worshipped Apollo, Mars, Jupiter and Minerva. But he is simply equating Gaulish deities with his own Roman gods, as indeed the Romans equated some of their gods with the gods of the Greeks. He does not give us a single Gaulish name. Other Latin and Greek authors do give us names and many other names are found in inscriptions dedicating monuments all over the vast area once dominated by the Celts, from Galatia in Asia Minor to Spain in the west.

We have more than four hundred names in all, and more than three hundred of them occur only once. It is evident that they are the names of local deities, each tribe or group of tribes having their special cult. Some of the names are worth mentioning here. The poet Lucan says that the three great gods of the Celts were Esus, Taranis and Teutates and each of these has a sort of echo in Irish tradition. The common Irish name Eogan means "born of Esus". Taranis sounds like the Irish word for thunder, *torann*. And Teutates seems to have been the title of the god of each tribe, not a proper name at all, for it is derived from the same root as the Irish word *tuath* "tribe"; and in Irish sagas, when a warrior takes an oath, he says, *tongim do dia tonges mo thuath*, "I swear by the god by whom my people swear", that is to say, by Teutates, the tribal god, or so we may suppose.

Another name is important, that of the Irish Lug of the Long Arm. It occurs in Switzerland as a plural *Lugoues*, and is common in the place-name Lugudunum which occurs in a great many places in Europe. It is the name of Lyons and London and Leon in France, of Leiden in Holland and Liegnity in Silesia. This Lug must have been prominent among the gods of the Celts, but we do not know what his special character was. He is the god of Lugnasad, the 1st of August, which was, I suppose, a harvest festival, and Lug may have been a god of fertility. Maire Mac Neill has recently shown, in a remarkable book, that the tradition of Lugnasad survived in the observance of Garland Sunday in many parts of Ireland until our own time. The sun and the moon, thunder and lightning, rain and fertility, birth and death, health and sickness, these were powers or concepts that a man had to conciliate, and we can be sure that they were all provided for, but without written records, we cannot tell whether any of the gods, whose names we know, was specially associated with one or other of them. Various guesses have been made, not without some foundation, but it would be tedious to discuss them here.

There is one element, the most important to a pagan, of which more can be said, namely the Earth herself, as a source of fertility. Many primitive peoples regarded the earth as a mother—we often speak of "mother earth"— and the Celts worshipped her in triple form under the title *matres* or *matrones*. The dedications that survive on monuments in Gaul are in Latin, and the figures are sometimes represented with baskets of fruit or horns of plenty, or with children in their laps. They may have been goddesses of birth as well as of fertility, and this notion appears too in Irish and Welsh tradition. There is a Welsh place-name, *Y Foel Famau*, "The Hill of the Mothers", and in Co. Kerry, The Paps are *Dá Chích nAnann*, which are mentioned in Cormac's glossary. Cormac says that Anu was the mother of the Gods and that she fed them well. She was then probably a goddess of birth and fertility.

Another feature of Celtic religion which emerges clearly is that wells, rivers, and sacred trees were objects of devotion and had patron gods or goddesses. Indeed, certain rivers seem to have been themselves divine. There was a sanctuary to the *dea Sequana* at the source of the river Seine and one to the *dea Matrona* near to the source of the Marne. In Ireland, the Boyne was a goddess and the mother of Oengus; and there were sacred trees in many places in Ireland. There is a special word, *bile*, for a sacred tree. And then there were animal-gods in Gaul, the bull, *Taruos*, and the mare, *Epona*, and the bear, *Artos*. In Ireland the bull-god survives in shadowy form in the great Táin, where the Brown Bull of Cualnge and the Whitehorned Bull seem to be supernatural beings, though they have lost a good deal of their sacred character in the telling of the saga.

The priests who maintained the cult of these gods were

the druids, and Caesar tells us a good deal about them.
They conducted the private and public sacrifices. They
taught that the soul was immortal and passed after
death into another body, rather as the Hindus believed.
They also thought that all men were descended from
the god of the Underworld, and they were learned in
astronomy and natural history.

After a victory the captured animals were sacrificed
to the god of war. At a private sacrifice or at the regular
feasts of the year, the victim was perhaps a ram or a
bull or a bird, but we know little about Gaulish feasts
or ritual, as the druids themselves have left no written
records. Sometimes human victims were sacrificed, and
Caesar says that criminals were preferred, as being more
pleasing to the gods, but that, failing them, even innocent
victims were chosen.

We may turn to the Irish sources for more information,
and the sources here are plentiful, but they are very
difficult to interpret because we have them only in
sagas handed down by Christian monks. The wonder is
that the good monks have told us so much.

O'Rahilly, in his great book on *Early Irish History and
Mythology*, finds in Irish tradition a basic myth, the
slaying of an Otherworld God, who is also the Sun-God,
by a Hero, and the god is slain with his own weapon.
The Otherworld God is the Dagda or Eochaid Ollathair
or Dian Cécht or Balor or Aed (a name which means
"fire"); and the hero is Lug, who slays Balor, or Cú
Chulainn, who slays a dog-god, or Finn, who slays Goll
or Aed, or Cormac Mac Airt, whom O'Rahilly regards
as an avatar of Lug, "who, in one of his functions was
the divine prototype of human kingship". The weapon
is the thunderbolt or lightning, represented by a flashing
sword, the *Claidheamh Soluis* of folklore. O'Rahilly may
be right in these speculations, but he had not time to
reduce them to order. Indeed, Gerard Murphy, in his
important introduction to the third volume of *Dunaire
Finn*, arrives at conclusions about Finn which support

O'Rahilly's interpretation. But the myth that O'Rahilly here traces may not be Celtic at all and may lie in a deeper stratum of tradition. The legend of the Golden Bough, which Frazer chose as the title for his great work, is of a king killed with his own weapon, by the hero who succeeds him.

One observation of O'Rahilly's is worth noting, because it has a bearing on what I said about the Gaulish gods. He says that the Otherworld God had many aspects or functions: he was a god of the Sun and of Thunder and Lightning and the ancestor of mankind. (Zeus, the god of the sky and father of men, is a Greek analogy.) And he points out that the tendency to departmentalise gods as gods of war, hunting, healing, fertility and so on, is partly the legacy of Greece, and not of general application. The Dagda (the Good God) of Irish tradition seems to have had various functions and may have had various names, Ollathair, Dian Cécht, Eochu and so on, to describe them.

I have now given you a good many Irish names and it is time to come closer to the Irish sources—to consider what we know about Irish, as distinct from Celtic, religion. The main dynasty of Irish gods was known as *Tuatha Dé Danann*, "Peoples of the Goddess Danu". Their chief was the Dagda, or Good God, whom we have already met, and who had other names as well. He was the lover of Boann, the river Boyne, and their son was Oengus. Other male gods were Lug and Midir and Nuadu of the Silver Arm and Cú Roé and Dond, who was god of the Underworld and sometimes thought of as the father of men. The array of goddesses is not very satisfying. Boann was one and there were Bé Find and Étain and Macha and Bodb, who was a raven-goddess associated with death. These gods were supposed to live in sacred mounds, really ancient burial-mounds of pre-Celtic times, as we now know. New Grange is one of these and it has recently been discovered that there was another at Tara. Indeed, the whole of Meath is an

area of pre-Celtic grave-mounds, from the Lough Crew
Hills to the Boyne Valley. But there were other gods
who lived beyond the sea or under the sea, Manannán
Mac Lir, Labraid Swift Hand on Sword and the goddess
Fand, and who seem to belong to a separate tradition;
and this tradition was common to Wales and Ireland,
for the Welsh Manawyddan fab Llyr is certainly the
Irish Manannán, though of course one may be simply
a borrowing of the other.

The *Tuatha Dé Danann* were supposed to have
defeated another group of supernatural beings called
Fomuire or Fomorians, who may originally have been
dwellers beyond or under the sea. But O'Rahilly regards
them all as one, Balor, King of the Fomorians, who was
slain by Lug of the *Tuatha Dé Danann*, being simply
one form of the Otherworld God. The truth is that
scholars have not yet arrived at a clear understanding
of Irish mythology, but there is plenty of material, as
O'Rahilly shows.

Nothing is known about the religious practises of the
ancient Irish, about sacrifices or forms of worship, any
more than of the Gauls. There are, indeed, references
to human sacrifice in both areas and it may well be
that such gruesome rites took place in times of imminent
disaster. There is an account of an idol, *Crom Cruaich*,
to which sacrifice was offered at Samain (November 1st)
and we are told that St. Patrick destroyed the idol and
forbade the rite. But it would seem to be a relic of
barbarism that has little to do with the gods we know
about. Divination was practised by the druids of Gaul,
who foretold the future by watching the flight of birds,
by examining their entrails and so on. (The Roman
augurs and soothsayers sought omens in similar ways.)
And these practices were also common in Ireland. We
have an interesting description of one such rite of
divination in the saga of the *Wasting Sickness of Cú
Chulainn*. It is called *tarbfeis*, "bull-feast", and is said to
have been a means of choosing a king. The saga is mere

legend, but the passage may preserve the tradition of a means of divination that was used:

"This is how that bull-feast used to be made: to kill a white bull, and for one man to eat his fill of its flesh and of its broth, and to sleep after that meal, and for four druids to chant a spell of truth over him. And the form of the man to be made king used to be shown to him in a dream, his shape and his description, and the manner of work that he was doing. The man awoke out of his sleep, and told his dream to the king, a young warrior, noble and strong, with two red circles around his body, standing over the pillow of a sick man in Emain Macha". There was doubtless a lot of this simple magic, and traces of it may be found in modern folklore. Human memory records various practices of the kind I have in mind, for instance, the sacrifice of a cock at the building of a new house, the placing of a live coal under the churn to ensure the coming of butter, and the knocking over of chairs when a corpse is leaving the house. These are, after all, propitiatory rites, but they hardly deserve to be called religion.

The Celts of Gaul and of Ireland certainly believed in an afterlife, that man survived in some sense after death, for they buried food containers and food and other provisions with their dead. Archaeology tells us that much. And the written sources tell us more. For Gaul we have the evidence of Julius Caesar, who says that the druids teach that souls do not die but pass from one to another after death: and this is confirmed by verses of the poet Lucan who says of the druids: "From you we learn that the spirit animates the body in another world. If your songs are true, death is only the centre of a long life".

We have seen that the Irish believed in an Otherworld, sometimes called the Land of the Young or the Delightful Plain, and imagined as somewhere on islands beyond the sea or under the sea. Some heroes are allowed to visit it during their lives, *Bran* and *Conla* and *Cú*

Chulainn and *Oisín,* and some never return. There is a poem in which *Donn,* the god of the dead, says "All of you shall come to my house after your death". And perhaps D'Arbois and O'Rahilly are right in the opinion that the belief of the Celts was that after death they went to the house of their ancestor, the god of the Otherworld.

The gods were supernatural powers which you tried to get on your side or which you feared to offend. The French scholar, Fontenelle said long ago: "For all divinities imagined by the pagans, the dominant idea is that of power, and they had little or no regard to wisdom or justice. They imagined their gods at a time when gods had nothing more precious to offer than power, and they imagined them in forms which bore the marks of power rather than of wisdom."

There were religious festivals in Ireland and we know something about them. There were four great feasts of the year. *Imbolg* (February 1st), *Beltaine* (May 1st), *Lugnasad* (August 1st) and *Samain* (November 1st). Of these *Samain* was the greatest and *Beltaine* the next. *Samain* was supposed to mean "the end of summer", but Vendryes suggests that it may be derived from *sam,* meaning "one" or "together", which occurs in Latin *semel* and *similis.* At any rate it was a great feast, when the barrier between this world and the Otherworld was removed and contact with the gods was close. It was on this day that the feast of Tara was held, and Professor Binchy has made it probable that this was the inaugural feast of the King of Tara held only once in his reign and celebrating his ritual marriage with Sovereignty.

This is one ancient religious belief that we do grasp clearly, namely, that sovereignty (*flaithes*) was believed to be a *puissance,* a supernatural force, imagined as female, to which the king must be wedded, if his reign was to prosper. The ritual was even called *banais ríg,* the king's wedding; it was the *hieros gamos,* or sacred marriage of Greek tradition and was, of course, a fertility rite. Giraldus Cambrensis reported an account he had heard of the inauguration of an Irish king, even after the Norman invasion, involving symbolic marriage with a mare, a rite which resembles the ancient horse-sacrifice of the Hindus and seems to be a survival, not merely of Celtic religion, but of ancient Indo-European tradition. We are reminded of the Greek cult of Poseidon and Demeter, who was mother earth; and they were honoured in the forms of horse and mare. The mating is of a god and goddess in Greece and of a king with a goddess in Ireland, but there is a common element of mythology. Poseidon, too, by the way, had many names, Hippios, Melanthos, Asphaleios and so on; as god of horses and chariots, of earthquakes and the underworld, of the sea, and as father of men.

Of the other three feasts I have little to say. Of *Imbolc* we know little. In Christian times it was associated with the lambing season, but it may have been a time for ceremonies of purification like the Roman lustrations. *Beltaine* was May Day, the summer festival which is a day of celebration elsewhere than in Ireland, and *Lugnasad* had as patron the god Lug. We know that games and races were held on these festive occasions and the *oenach* or assembly was held then, too, when perhaps the king issued ordinances and arbitrated cases in dispute with the advice of a jurist.

There is one concept in Irish tradition which has to do with religion, or with magic, namely, the *geis*, which is an absolute prohibition from doing certain things. These *gessa* may be quite arbitrary and they vary with individuals. Sometimes they seem to be related to the totem-cult, as when Cú Chulainn ("Culann's Hound") may not eat the flesh of a dog, or *Diarmait*, whose life-span was united to that of a boar, may not join in a boar-hunt, or *Conaire*, whose father was a bird, may not kill birds. Sometimes they appear to be motivated by the avoidance of a set of circumstances which had formerly led to disaster. In some cases a *geis* is imposed by one man upon another, often by means of a successful exploit, as when Cú Chulainn lays a *geis* upon the Connachtmen, binding them not to pass the ford until a single warrior has removed the branch he has thrust into the ground. In some cases the *geis* seems to be quite accidental, a decree of fate. The basis of *geis* is honour. If a man violates his *geis* he loses honour, but violation of a *geis* involves also material ruin. The penalty is not stated, but in the sagas it is often death.

And then there was the practice of fasting as a means of redress, which is common to Ireland and to India. (It is not therefore specially Celtic, but rather an ancient Indo-European custom. Only the Celts preserved it in this part of the world.) If a man had wronged you, you went to his house with witnesses, and remained there fasting—on hunger-strike—until you obtained redress of the wrong. This practice was fully recognised by law and indeed it plays an important part in the Brehon law-tracts that survive.

We are passing from religion into the realm of social organisation, from the first to the second part of my subject. We know that there were kings in Ireland. In Gaul too there were once kings and the Gaulish word for king, *rix*, is common to personal names, Dumnorix, *rí an domhain* or "king of the world", Vercingetorix, and the tribe of Bituriges "kings of the world". But the era of kingship was passing when Caesar entered Gaul, and powerful tribes such as the Helvetii, the Aedui and the Arvetni were governed by an aristocracy without a king. Caesar tells us that in Gaul, society was divided into three classes, *druides*, *equites* and *plebs*, and this stratification of society is valid for Ireland (*fili, faith, aithech*) and probably for Wales as well. He tells us that the druids underwent a very long period of training, twenty years, and that instruction was oral. The druids avoided the use of writing to preserve their tradition, for writing was an innovation unfit for recording sacred learning. They were teachers and judges as well as priests, instructing the young men, settling private and public disputes, and practising divination by means of various rites. Like the brahmins in India, the druids were the highest class in society, and even kings could not make decisions or act without their approval, "so that in truth it was they who gave orders, the kings being merely their servants and ministers of their will".

Besides the druids, there were two other classes of learned men, *vates* and *bardi*, prophets and bards. All of this is fully confirmed by the evidence of Irish sources. The long training—in Ireland it lasted for 12 years:— the oral transmission of learning, and the exalted status of the druid. (We are told in the *Táin* that the king might not speak before the druid.) The Irish *druí*, *fáith* and *bard*, preserve the very same names. But in Christian Ireland the druids had been separated by function, and we find distinct professions of *fili* and *brithem*, the *fili* as poet, historian, genealogist and man of letters, the *brithem* as judge, and these two professions survived the coming of Christianity and continued to flourish, while the druid as pagan priest was, of course, doomed to extinction.

Dr. Binchy has described Irish society as tribal, rural, hierarchical, and familiar, and his account may be taken as true of Celtic society in general. The *tuath* was a relatively small area, in Ireland the size of a modern barony— though this must have varied in different counties— with its king, himself subject to an over-king, the nobles, who were not land-owners, for the land belonged to the family, but who had wealth in cattle; and the commoners, who tilled the soil, paid food-rent to the king, and received cattle from the lord to graze the land. Then there were slaves, who had no rights.

The important unit was the family, a group consisting of the descendants of a common great-grandfather, four generations, and known in Ireland as the *derbfine*. This was the normal property-owning unit, and it was also the unit for the purpose of dynastic succession. Any member of the king's *derbfine* was eligible to succeed him as king, his uncle or his brother or his nephew as well as his son. There was no legislature, no police, of course, no public administration of the law. But the old customary law was preserved, in memory, by the jurists and interpreted by them. If you refused to accept their decision, you were liable to be distrained upon by your neighbours and you had no remedy. Caesar tells us that in Gaul, persons who failed to comply with judicial decisions were excluded from the sacrifices and were deprived of honour and normal society. It was an ancient form of the boycott. And this was also true in Ireland.

There is one of Dr. Binchy's terms that may not be of general application to Celtic society, the term "rural". In ancient Ireland there were no towns, or even villages in the English sense. But on the continent there were defensible groups of dwellings, the *Oppida*, which offered resistance to the Roman advance. Ankara and Belgrade and Milan and Trier and Lyons are all old Celtic settlements, and they must have been fortified places in Celtic times.

And there is one other feature in which Gaul was ahead of Ireland and most of Britain, namely in the use of coinage, which they had learned from Greece and Rome.

The Celts were once a great and conquering people. They plundered Rome in the fourth century B.C., and Delphi in Greece in the third, spreading as far as Galatia in Asia Minor. The tide of fortune later turned against them and now the heirs to Celtic tradition survive only in Brittany and Wales and Scotland and Ireland. Like the Jews, it has been their destiny, for many centuries, to suffer wrongs rather than to inflict them. This is not an ignoble history, and the Celtic heritage is no mean tradition. It is a heritage of beauty in decorative art and in lyric poetry, of incandescent imagination in literature, of devotion to ideals rather than to material gain, of vitality and the will to survive, and indeed courage in battle too. "What was it that maintained you so in your lives?" St. Patrick asks of *Caoilte* in the *Colloquy of the Ancients*, and *Caoilte* answered: "Truth in our hearts, and strength in our arms, and fulfilment in our tongues".

This Celtic heritage is ours in a peculiar way, for we are the only independent people to possess it. We shall do well to cherish it.

PROFESSOR MYLES DILLON

THE CELTIC AFTERMATH
IN THE ISLANDS

In previous lectures in this series it has been explained how the Celtic peoples came to Britain and Ireland from the Continent; and how those who occupied Ireland were Goidels or Gaels, speaking the Goidelic variety of Celtic, whereas those who settled in Britain were Britons, speaking the Brittonic variety. Whether any Brittonic-speaking Celts ever came across to Ireland, and if so, where and in what numbers, is a vexed question; but this problem need not be discussed here, since if Brittonic was spoken in Ireland as well as Goidelic the difference was probably pretty well obliterated by the late Roman period where my subject begins, and the inhabitants of Ireland were doubtless almost all Gaelic in speech.

The early immigrations of Celts from the Continent into Ireland, and the well-known later invasions of the Normans, the English, and—in Ulster—the Scots give the impression that Ireland was always at the receiving end, that she was constantly on the defensive against assaults from outside, and never the reverse. In fact, however, there was a time—and this is partly what I am to deal with—when the Irish were themselves a colonising people. Let us look first at the situation of the Celtic nations in Britain and Ireland towards the end of the Roman period, say in the third century, as a starting-point for the consideration of these Irish colonial movements. In Ireland we have the Goidelic Celts, speaking Irish (with perhaps among them some non-Goidelic but Goidelicised Celts, also speaking Irish); and in England, Wales, and southern Scotland up to the northern of the two Roman Walls the British Celts,

73

speaking Brittonic. Beyond that Wall, north of the Forth and Clyde, we have a third people, the Picts, about whose origins and language I shall have something to say presently; it is enough for the moment to note that they were largely Celtic too, and probably close cousins of the Britons. The state of the Celtic peoples at the present day is of course very different from this in certain respects, and the roots of some of the differences go right back to the period which I am to discuss, and which has been called "the Celtic aftermath in the islands".

The Roman rule in Britain did at least protect the Romanised Britons, for some centuries, from foreign attack. But already in the fourth century we begin to hear of the incursions of the peoples called the Picts and Scots, as every schoolboy knows; and, as I suppose most people are aware, the word Scot did not at first mean at all what we mean by it—it meant an Irishman. How it came eventually to mean a man of Scotland is one of the points I am to discuss. The Picts and Scots, the latter coming across the sea from Ireland, appear to have entered into a confederation to attack Roman Britain as allies, and some disastrous joint raids were carried out at various times in the fourth century, notably the great attack of the year 368 which took the province at a disadvantage, devastated almost the whole of England, and seriously weakened the Roman position there. It was during one of these raids, a later one, that St. Patrick was carried off as a boy from Britain to Ireland, at the beginning of the fifth century. We hear little from Latin historians about the course of the Irish assaults on Britain, but other sources show that the "Scots" did not merely attack, they also settled down and founded colonies. There is some slight reason to think, though it is little more than an ingenious theory, that these colonies were actually formed with Roman encouragement or at any rate connivance. If the Romans, who had by now few troops to spare for the defence of Britain when they needed them badly to prop up or overthrow the tottering emperors nearer home—if they could bribe or flatter some of these bold raiders into setting up, at strategic points in Britain, as proud allies of the Empire, they would act as a buffer against further attacks and might themselves settle down peaceably and be satisfied with what they had got. It was setting a thief to catch a thief. Such is the theory, at least.

However that may be, it does seem clear that in the course of the fourth and fifth centuries a very considerable Irish colony was established in south-western Wales, particularly in Pembrokeshire, Carmarthenshire, and Cardiganshire, and a much weaker and more scattered one in North Wales, in Anglesea, Carnarvonshire, and Denbighshire. A third, again apparently a rather minor affair, was planted in parts of Cornwall and South Devon. There may, very probably, have been another in the Isle of Man at this time. At any rate, that island, which is geographically part of Britain, seems to have been British-speaking at first, but there were Irishmen there at least as early as the fifth century. It became a Gaelic-speaking country, and remained so until modern times. Thus, by the end of the Roman period the western approaches to Britain were occupied by and in the control of the Irish.

Various sources tell us something about how it happened. In the first place, there is a well-known passage in the Irish glossary compiled at the beginning of the tenth century by Cormac, king and bishop of Cashel, in which he says: "The power of the Irish over the Britons was great, and they had divided Britain between them into estates; . . . and the Irish lived as much east of the sea as they did in Ireland, and their dwellings and royal fortresses were made there. Hence is Dind Tradui, . . . that is, the triple rampart of Criomhthann . . . king of Ireland and Britain as far as the English Channel. . . . From this division originated the fort of the sons of Liathán in the lands of the Britons of Cornwall. . . . And

they were in that control for a long time, even after the
coming of St. Patrick to Ireland." It is not known where
Cormac learned this, and the tradition refers of course
to a period some five centuries before his time; but it is
circumstantial, and its broad outlines are confirmed by
other evidence. Nennius, the Welsh historian writing
about 100 years before Cormac, also speaks of the
sons of Liathán, and says they were settled in S. Wales,
in Pembrokeshire and the coast towards Swansea.
The "sons of Liathán" are the tribe of the Uí Liatháin
of East Cork, which shows where these colonists in the
south were believed to have come from. Actually this
is strikingly confirmed by the Irish story of the migration
of the Déise from County Waterford, just next-door to
the Uí Liatháin in Cork under their leader Eochaidh,
to south-west Wales late in the third century. The tale
includes a pedigree of the Irish kings of this part of Wales
for fourteen generations, from Eochaidh down to the
king reigning in the eighth century, when the writer
lived. The names of the later kings are Welsh; and the
striking thing is that we have elsewhere what is really
the same genealogy of the kings of south-west Wales
preserved in a purely Welsh source, and carried down to
the tenth century. It seems a certain fact that, at some
time in the late Roman period, considerable Irish
colonies from East Munster settled in South Wales,
Cornwall, and Devon, and that from one of them there
sprang a line of kings of south-west Wales who were still
ruling there in the tenth century.

We know much less about the colony in North Wales.
That it existed is certain, but Irish sources tell us nothing
about it. We must turn again to Welsh tradition. The
same Nennius speaks of Cunedda, a king from southern
Scotland, who came south with eight of his sons, drove
the Irish out of North Wales, and occupied it himself.
If the story is historical this expulsion must probably
have taken place in the middle of the fifth century.
Welsh tradition tells, however, of further struggles, in the

course of which Cunedda's grandson, Cadwallon, finally expelled the Irish from the North.

We have another source of information on all these colonies, including the Isle of Man; the Ogam inscriptions of Ireland. Widely scattered through the country, these are standing stones bearing inscriptions in an alphabet consisting of straight grooves and notches cut up the side of the stone, written in a very archaic stage of the Irish language. A considerable number of such inscriptions are found in Cornwall and Devon, South and North Wales, and the Isle of Man, exactly the places where the Irish settled, and it is obvious that they were erected by those settlers. Many of them have the same inscription given also in Latin letters, or some form of the same inscription; and it is possible to date them to the fifth, sixth, and early seventh centuries, thus providing us with evidence that the Irish colonists continued to be consciously Irish until at least as late as this. There is no doubt about that. One of these inscriptions, in Carmarthenshire, bears the name *Quenvendanos*. The *qᵘ* proves it is Irish, not British, and in fact it is a compound of *ceann*, "head" and *fionn*, "white", and would be *Ceannannán* in Modern Irish. Another monument not far away has the word *inigena* on it, Modern Irish *inghean*, "daughter". Still another, near Bodmin in Cornwall, is in memory of one *Dunocatus*, that is to say Donnchadh. Several include the word *aui*, Modern Irish *uí*, genitive of *ua*, "grandson". These inscriptions do not tell a story as Nennius and Cormac do; nevertheless they bear eloquent testimony to the widespread settlements of Irishmen in the western districts of Britain; and no one who sees these stones with their crumbling inscriptions still standing on the moors or in the tiny country churchyards of the west can help being moved by these mute witnesses to the Irishmen settled in Britain long ago.

I have yet to speak of the greatest and most successful of the Irish emigrations, one which did not fade away and is with us in Britain yet, the peopling of Gaelic

Scotland. There are tales in early Irish manuscripts which have been taken by some scholars to imply that this process had started as early as the third or fourth centuries. But the evidence for this is of a very unsatisfactory kind, and there is no good reason to suppose that the movement began before the famous invasion of the Sons of Erc towards the end of the fifth century. They came from the small kingdom of Dál Riada in Antrim and occupied what is now the county of Argyll, to which they gave the same name, Dál Riada. The subsequent history of the rise of this little colony would take too long to trace. Everyone knows how St. Columba came from Ireland in 563 and founded his monastery in Iona to minister to the needs of the Gael in Scotland and to convert the Picts. Already, by this time Scottish Dál Riada under its great king Aodhán mac Gabhráin, was extending his control eastwards into the country of the Picts. For the next two and a half centuries the history of Scottish Dál Riada was a series of battles and campaigns, with varying fortunes, against her powerful neighbours, the Picts in the east, the Britons in the south-west, and the Northumbrian English in the south-east. Then, in the middle of the ninth century the Pictish resistance crumbled; Dál Riada under Kenneth mac Alpine absorbed all of Pictland, and the whole of Scotland north of the Forth and Clyde became one Gaelic kingdom over which the Gaelic language and civilisation quickly spread. It was now called Scotia or Scotland, the land of the Irishmen, as the name really meant; but the Irish in Ireland had given up calling themselves Scots by now, and their country had always been Éire, so that eventually the words Scotia and Scot acquired the meaning they now bear—the land and people of Scotland.

There is no need to deal with the further history of Gaelic Scotland, except to say that in the course of the tenth and eleventh centuries its kings acquired those parts, of what is now Scotland, which lie south of the Forth and Clyde, and that in consequence of this the whole of Scotland became for a time Gaelic or partly Gaelic in speech. Some parts of the Highlands and almost all the Hebrides still speak Gaelic, of course, and the rest did so until recently; but a considerable amount of Gaelic must have been spoken for a time not only in, for instance, Aberdeenshire and Kincardineshire and Fife but also as far south as the English border. This state of affairs did not last very long, for Gaelic was driven back again towards the Highlands during the twelfth and thirteenth centuries, but the undoubted traces of it are still plainly to be seen in the form of place-names given by the Gaelic Scots who settled in these wide lands. Names like Achingall, *achadh na nGall*, "the field of the foreigners", or Kilduff, *coill dubh*, "the black wood", south-east of Edinburgh, or Fingland near Peebles, *fionn ghleann*, "the bright glen", and scores of others, are clear evidence of this. The Irish colony in western Scotland had a very different fate from those in Wales and western England, and it has given to Scotland a permanent Gaelic inheritance.

Meanwhile, what of the Picts, the people of Scotland north of the Forth and east of the Grampians? As we see them in the period when we know them, between late Roman times and the middle of the ninth century, they maintained their independence against the Britons of the south, the Scots of Dál Riada, and the English of Northumbria, in a continual series of battles. They had by no means the worst of this. For instance, we find them annihilating the army of the king of Northumbria at Nechtansmere in Angus—*Linn Garan*, "the Pool of the Crane", as they probably called it themselves—in 685; or, under their great king Unuist, sacking the capital of Dál Riada at Dunadd in Argyll in 736. Finally their language and civilisation disappeared before the encroachments of the Irish Scots in the ninth century, and we know very little about these things. The ruling classes seem to have been definitely Celtic, speaking a P-Celtic language, very like British. There is some slight reason to think it may have differed somewhat from British, and that these Picts were not Britons so much as another group of Celts closely related to them; but this is quite uncertain. At any rate there does seem good cause to believe that the people of Pictland were not all Celts by any means; that a considerable element of an older, aboriginal, non-Celtic race survived among them, speaking a non-Celtic language unintelligible to us; and that the civilisation of the ruling Celtic Picts was much influenced by that of these older tribes. There was a curious custom whereby the succession to the throne, and doubtless to other inheritances, passed in Pictland not from father to son but from father to sister's son, in other words always through the female line instead of the succession through the male line to which we are accustomed. This seems to be a consequence of a primitive stage of polyandry, for which there is some evidence—and polyandry is not a Celtic practice. Further traces of these pre-Celtic Picts are seen in the extraordinary and certainly non-Celtic names of some of the ancient legendary kings, such as Bliesblituth and Uipoignamet; and particularly in the inscriptions on tombstones. The Picts learned the Ogam alphabet from the Irish of Dál Riada, and set up a considerable number of inscriptions in the eighth and ninth centuries; but they are in a language which nobody can interpret. Why should they write their epitaphs in what seems to have been the language of the subjected pre-Celtic natives? Speculation is vain, but one may perhaps suggest that it had acquired some superstitious or magic significance for the Celtic Picts, which induced them to use it for such semi-religious purposes, Christians though they were.

Pictish civilisation is an extraordinarily interesting subject. So little is known about them, and yet enough is known to raise great curiosity. One mystery still unsolved is the strange figure-carvings on tombstones found widely scattered in many parts of Pictland. They belong to much the same period as the Ogam inscriptions. They represent certain fixed motifs which appear again and again—a decorated crescent with a kind of V-shaped flowered sceptre behind it; a snake; a fish; an object like a pair of spectacles; and a number of others, all carved on the stone with an incredible artistic mastery. What they mean no one knows, whether they are clan symbols or status-symbols referring to the dead man, or what; but one cannot look at them without seeing that this is the work of a very high artistic tradition.

I have left to the last the Britons of southern Britain. Deserted by the might of Rome early in the fifth century, they were exposed to the incursions, not merely of Picts from Scotland and Scots from Ireland, but also of Germanic Angles, Saxons and Jutes from Denmark and Holland. Everyone knows the story of Hengist and Horsa, and how the invading English gradually overran Britain and subdued the Britons. Between their arrival in the middle of the fifth century and the end of the seventh or beginning of the eighth they gradually occupied the whole of England (leaving only Wales and Cornwall), and much of southern Scotland up to the Forth and Clyde. Cornwall was taken in the course of the ninth century, but the English there can never have been numerous, and the British language lived on in Cornwall throughout the Middle Ages, not finally fading out until the eighteenth century. Wales maintained its political independence to the thirteenth century, but of course it has remained a Celtic country culturally to the present day. South-eastern and much of south-western Scotland was English for several centuries, and Edinburgh was an English capital before it was a Scottish one. Hence the Lothian country especially is full of Anglo-Saxon place-names of an early type, such as Haddington—the kind of name one might expect to find in a thoroughly English area like Sussex. But they could never win the country of the Britons of Strathclyde, the Clyde basin south of Glasgow, and it was the Gaelic

Scots who absorbed this kingdom in the end in the eleventh century, not the English. Meanwhile the Strathclyde Britons continued independent, speakers of a language virtually identical with Welsh. Indeed they even extended their kingdom far into England for a time, well into Cumberland and up to the top of the Pennines on the border of Yorkshire. As a result, the proportion of Brittonic place-names in northern Cumberland is very distinctly higher than in any other part of England apart from Cornwall and a couple of patches on the Welsh border. Penrith, Welsh *penn rhyd*, "the head of the ford", is a well-known instance. British place-names and river-names are to be found in most parts of England—the various rivers Avon, which is Welsh *afon*, "river", form a good example—and they constitute proof that the Anglo-Saxons did not entirely exterminate the Britons, as was once thought, but must have settled down beside them and intermarried with them. It is noticeable, however, that there are far fewer of them in the east of England than in the centre and west, and it does look very much as if the early stages of the Anglo-Saxon conquest did result in the disappearance of much, if not most, of the native population in the east.

As the Saxons pressed westwards in southern England large numbers of the Britons made up their minds to emigrate while they still could, rather than become enslaved. In the fifth, sixth and seventh centuries, but especially in the late sixth, they fled from Britain and settled down in Brittany, opposite Cornwall and Devon. There is some reason to think that a very large number of them must have come from Devon, for whereas Cornwall remained fundamentally a Celtic country for centuries, Devon became thoroughly English very early; British place-names are not commoner in Devon than they are in Dorset and Somerset and Wiltshire, and hence it is believed that the county was only thinly populated with Britons when the English got there. In Brittany the emigrants founded great colonies and turned the peninsula into a British country, destined to play a notable part in the history of France. They kept their British language, which is still the speech of the Bretons; it is closely related to Cornish. They called their northern coast Domnonia, the name of the Devon from which they came; but there must have been a good many Cornishmen among them, since the central and south-western part of Brittany became *Kerneo*, which is simply "Cornwall".

We began with the Goidelic branch of the Celtic people settled in the whole of Ireland and the Brittonic and Pictish branches in the whole of Britain. The causes which brought about the very different state of affairs, which we know in mediaeval and modern times, were two:—the migrations of the Irish eastwards into Britain and especially into Scotland, and the migration of the Anglo-Saxons westwards there and especially into England. The Irish have remained in Ireland and the English in England, but the Celtic world between them had become, by Norman times, a more or less narrow fringe: the Highland Scots, the faint traces of the Strathclyde Britons, the Manx, the Welsh, the Cornish, and an exiled offshoot from southern Britain in Brittany. This situation has remained substantially unaltered till the present day. It was formed during the post-Roman Dark Ages, in consequence of movements which may well be called part of "the Celtic aftermath in the islands".

PROFESSOR KENNETH JACKSON

THE COURSE OF IRISH HISTORY
Edited by T.W. Moody and F.X. Martin

The first of its kind in its field, this book provides a rapid short survey, with a geographical introduction, of the whole course of Ireland's history. Based on the series of television programmes first transmitted by Radio Telefís Éireann from January to June 1966, it is designed to be both popular and authoritative, concise but comprehensive, highly selective but balanced and fair-minded, critical but constructive and sympathetic. A distinctive feature is its wealth of illustrations.

The present edition is a revised and enlarged version of the original book. A new chapter has been added, bringing the narrative to the end of 1982, and the illustrations have been correspondingly augmented. The list of books for further reading has been expanded into a comprehensive bibliography of modern writings on Irish history. The chronology has been rewritten, updated, and much enlarged, so that it now amounts to a substantial supplement to the text. Finally, the index has been revised and extended both to include the new chapter and to fill gaps in the original coverage.

THE FENIAN MOVEMENT
Edited by T.W. Moody

This book is an introduction to the history of the secret revolutionary movement for Irish independence that emerged out of the wreck of the Young Ireland rising of 1848. The movement appeared to have spent itself in the futile rising of 1867, but in fact it persisted despite baffling difficulties and discouragements for half a century, and found its fulfilment in the Easter rising of 1916. The subject is presented in three parts: (1) an account of dual origin of the Fenian movement in Ireland and America, of the rising of 1867, and of the later history of Fenianism to 1916; (2) a series of portraits of the seven dominant personalities in the movement – Stephens, Luby, O'Mahony, Devoy, O'Leary, Kickham, and O'Donovan Rossa; and (3) an assessment of the character and achievement of Fenianism and of its place in Irish history.

A Select bibliography of the historical writing and the source-materials on the subject is appended.

SIX GENERATIONS
Life and Work in Ireland from 1790
L.M. Cullen

Six generations represent only a short moment in the long history of human civilisation, but these six generations have brought more change in the way of life of the ordinary man and woman than came in the thousands of years before. From earliest times to the days of O'Connell, the speed of travel was no faster than that of a galloping horse; news of great events could take days even weeks to reach from one end of the country to another. This book describes the significant changes in everyday life – food, entertainment, household goods, working conditions, medicine, roads and communication – and what brought them about.

For the older generation this book will recall a way of life in the countryside which has virtually disappeared and for the younger generation it will illuminate what life was like while historic events such as the '98 rising, O'Connell's repeal movement, the Fenians and 1916 were being enacted. For both parents and pupils, this book will serve as a useful companion to the Telefís Scoile series of the same title.

MILESTONES IN IRISH HISTORY
Edited by Liam de Paor

Milestones in Irish History spans the whole range of time from early prehistory to the present, opening with Frank Mitchell's enquiry into the social and historical meaning of the building of the remarkable cemetery of megalithic tombs centred on the great monuments of Knowth, Dowth and Newgrange. Liam de Paor looks at the background and work of St. Patrick; Donnchadh Ó Corráin deals with Brian Boru and the Battle of Clontarf and Michael Richter examines the advent of the Normans.

Margaret MacCurtain discusses the Flight of the Earls and this is balanced, as it were, by an investigation of the new order that was created in its place in Aidan Clarke's look at the Plantations of Ulster. The Act of Union which made Ireland part of the United Kingdom in 1801 is examined by James McGuire and Kevin B. Nowlan looks at the career of Daniel O'Connell and Catholic Emancipation.

R.B. Walsh traces the decline of the Irish language and Donal McCartney examines the efforts to revive it at the turn of the century. Joseph Lee analyses the long drawn out struggle over the possession of land and Ronan Fanning gives his views on the partitioning of Ireland. John A. Murphy concludes with a look at the meaning of Ireland's entry to the EEC.

IRISH SAGAS
Edited by Myles Dillon

In Ireland, as in Wales, poetry and legend are the substance of the literature, and these essays will serve as an introduction to the prose tales of ancient Ireland. From these heroic sagas emerges a picture of an old Celtic society, recorded in manuscripts dating from the 8th century, indicating patterns of custom, social observances and fantasy, which may also be traced in the stories of other cultures.

Professor Dillon chose his team of collaborators with great care. Through their vivid translations they reconstruct the worlds of the mythological cycle, with stories of the pre-Christian gods; the Ulster cycle of heroic tales of great warriors; the Fenian cycle of inspiring noble youth; and the kingly cycle in which some historical figures have been vested with the immortality of legend.

Eleven top-flight Irish scholars give depth, background and new relevance to what is now accepted as the most important of Irish prose literature, recorded before historians, orators, dramatists and novelists took over the literary scene.

THE CELTS